Stepping Stones to Christian Maturity

by

Howard Booth

And so we shall all come together to that oneness in our faith and in our knowledge of the Son of God; we shall become mature people, reaching to the very height of Christ's full stature. Ephesians 4:13 (Good News Bible)

Other books by Howard Booth

On Parade!
Epworth Press, 1964

Prayer Tools for Health and Healing
The Grail, 1978

In Search of Health and Wholeness (Editor)
Division of Social Responsibility, 1984

Healing Experiences
Bible Reading Fellowship, 1985

Healing IS Wholeness
Division of Social Responsibility &
The Churches' Council for Health & Healing, 1987

Healing Through Caring,
a six week Bible based Study Course in Pastoral Care,
Arthur James, 1989

Booklets

The Christian Nurse
MacMillan, 1962

Growing in Christian Confidence,
Methodist Publishing House, 1986

STEPPING STONES
TO
CHRISTIAN MATURITY

by

HOWARD BOOTH

Arthur James
BOOK PUBLISHERS

STEPPING STONES TO CHRISTIAN MATURITY

First published in 1991

© Howard Booth, 1991

All rights reserved by Arthur James Limited, London

British Library Cataloguing in Publication Data
Booth, Howard
 Stepping Stones to Christian Maturity.
 1. Christianity. Religious Life.
 I. Title
 248.4

ISBN 0 85305 297 2

Cover design by The Creative House, Saffron Walden, Essex.

Made and printed in Great Britain by
The Guernsey Press Co. Ltd, Guernsey, Channel Islands.

ACKNOWLEDGEMENTS

My thanks to the responsible officers in the Bible Reading Fellowship and The Grail for their encouragement to proceed with this new and enlarged edition.

H.B.

NOTE

It is inevitable when writing a devotional book about making progress in the Christian life that, occasionally, similar ideas and thoughts recur but set within a different context. I hope that this serves to underline their importance.

H.B.

Details of books mentioned in the text are given at the end of the book.

THE AUTHOR

Howard Booth has just retired from being the Adviser on Health and Healing Ministries to the Division of Social Responsibility of the Methodist Church. He spent forty years in pastoral charge of Churches and Circuits. He has been widely used as a speaker at conferences, retreats, seminars, etc. dealing with health and healing issues and the development of the inner life. Side by side with this ministry, he has produced a number of books and booklets which have facilitated fellowship, discussion and sharing and which have helped many in the cultivation of their own inner lives. Currently he is Vice-chairman of The Churches' Council for Health and Healing.

CONTENTS

Each chapter contains reflections on its theme word with questions to stimulate discussion and sharing. In addition there are seven 'meditative style' daily Bible readings following each of the reflections, thus providing additional material both for personal devotion and further sharing.

The first five chapters were originally published in 1980 jointly by the Bible Reading Fellowship and The Grail. Chapters six to ten with their questions and daily readings are new.

INTRODUCTION

My wife, Alice, and I were walking a pathway alongside Waldon Beck in the Yorkshire Dales. As we ascended higher it became necessary to cross the water from time to time in order to make progress. Others had been before and there were always convenient stepping stones if you looked for them. But the stream was flowing strongly and was a little hazardous in places. We both lost our footing at least once and then discovered that the art of crossing successfully was to make sure that the stepping stone in front of you was secure and would hold you before you put your full weight upon it. But you could not always make absolutely sure and, in any case, it was exciting to take a minor risk and step out boldly.

Eventually we left the beck behind and set out across the moors. Our destination was the top of Buckden Pike and, when we arrived, there was a warm sense of satisfaction in having achieved our objective. We came down by a different route but eventually reached Waldon Beck again. The stepping stones were still there and we crossed to and fro several times. On our return journey we did not fall into the water. Our previous experience gave us confidence and we moved from stepping stone to stepping stone more easily.

As I reflected later on this experience I thought of the movement and development of my own Christian life. In order to get anywhere I have had to take some risks. As I have stepped out into the unknown I have felt the stone beneath my foot begin to wobble. From time to time I have slipped and got my feet wet! But this experience has proved invaluable! Further along the way I have succeeded where previously I had failed.

Some of these 'stepping stones' I now share with you in this book. The first five chapters with their associated readings have been published before and, when a new edition was suggested, it was decided that I might with profit add five more chapters and so double it in size. These have now been completed and I now offer you ten 'stepping stones' instead of five.

I hope that the book will have a variety of uses: personal reading and prayer, Lent groups and house fellowships either attached to one local Church or to a Council of Churches.

I trust that these 'stepping stones' will bear your weight and that you will step out boldly. There is no substitute for direct experience and no better way of gaining insight into life's meaning and purpose than reflecting upon it, seeking God's help through prayer and meditation, and then sharing your insights (and difficulties) with fellow travellers. As I have prepared my material I have discovered that all these 'stepping stones' are to be discovered again and again in that conversation piece between God and ourselves we call the Bible.

The first edition was dedicated to Alice, "with whom it is always a delight to travel up hill and down dale". I am happy to be able to do the same with this second edition and am thankful to tell my readers that it still is!

HOWARD BOOTH

1 AWARENESS

A new life begins in the closest and most intimate act of all human relationships. Then it enjoys the safety and warmth of a mother's body until the time of the birth when 'it' becomes he or she and emerges to a biologically separate existence. There follows a process of development which includes dependence, imitation and a progressive movement towards the discovery of self-identity. In the early weeks and months the physical contact with mother and father is all important. Nestling at the breast to feed is emotionally as well as biologically rewarding. Being picked up and held securely by loving arms is another high point of an infant's satisfaction.

As children experiment with physical movements so they begin to play emotional games as well. They discover how to get their physical needs met and eventually see how far they can manipulate their parents. They are looking for a sensible love on which they can depend. It is this trusting attitude which is going to be so important for their later development. If they do not find it for one reason or another then they are likely to lose their self-esteem. They may come to feel 'bad' inside if their legitimate desires for love and recognition are denied. The consequence will probably be that they are made to feel unworthy of being loved.

When this inner struggle is carried over into adolescence and adulthood the negative feelings are likely to be reinforced. Fierce desires for acceptance and recognition may be frightening to those who surround them and cause rejection. So the 'cycle of deprivation' continues and they may retreat within themselves and become withdrawn and perhaps depressed or they may develop aggressive tendencies which arise out of their desire to get back at those who will not allow them to be the kind of people they want to be.

This is then most likely to lead to an ongoing failure in personal relationships. Other people are viewed with suspicion; legitimate criticism is unbearable and rejection of any kind a nightmare. So in order to protect themselves against such emotional pain they live narrow, circumscribed lives which take no risks in their dealings with other people and consequently life is endured rather than enjoyed.

MOTHER CHURCH

This experience can be so easily repeated in their relationship with God and with the Church. They may look to Mother Church for the emotional satisfaction they have failed to find in human relationships. Religion can then become an escape from the realities of life and if this does not work then faith in God is discarded as being of no practical value. There may however be another outcome: someone like this may become totally dependent upon 'spiritual support' in a drugged kind of way which gives rise to a need for constant 'injections' of religious enthusiasm in one or other of its many forms.

IS THIS YOU?

You may well feel that what I have written above does not apply to you at all; you are not familiar in any way with the kind of experiences I have described. On the other hand there may well have been parts of it which you recognise within yourself. You may even now be conscious of failures in relationships which have spoilt and scarred your life. You may also feel rising up from deep inside you now and then fierce desires to be recognised, wanted, appreciated and accepted.

Religion is for most of us a varied experience. At times we just seem to be going through the motions while at others, worship and personal prayer are realities which give meaning and significance to life and without which we cannot do. Our attitudes towards the institutional church run along the same lines. Sometimes the support and inspiration we receive from the church is an essential part of our existence; at other times we feel it lets us down because it asks more from us than we are prepared to give.

My own experience in pastoral work leads me to believe that many people are like this. I know that I am myself an amalgam of faith and fear; of doubt and trust. I can enjoy most relationships but there are some which give me serious trouble and cause me great concern.

THE EXPERIENCE OF SOLITUDE

Awareness of ourselves and our own inner workings can be facilitated by skilled counselling or, at a deeper level, by psychotherapy. This requires an engagement in a relationship with a counsellor or therapist in which your own life's experiences are exposed, examined and reflected upon. The relationship established is of vital importance and out of the intimate dialectic which takes place a growing self-awareness is developed which can be a healing and liberating experience.

While not in any way de-valuing the help that can be given by such skilled people, it is quite impossible for many of us to have this kind of assistance. There is insufficient trained help available — and it is expensive. More important, it is not necessary for everyone. There are other ways of making progress in self-awareness.

One of these is to cultivate the discipline of a quiet mind; to make provisions for periods of creative solitude when we can listen in to what is going on deep inside ourselves and reflect upon it.

It is not easy. Just as sometimes we feel a need to fill our life with activity in order to stifle our inner pain, so sometimes we encourage an over-active mind in order to prevent us from taking an honest look at the darker side of our natures. Some form of meditation is a positive stepping stone to creative reflection. This can begin by concentrating upon a word, an idea or even an object. The aim is inner stillness and the discovery of the ability just to exist rather than to exist through activity, be it mental or physical. If and when this is achieved, reflection can then take place during which one faces up to serious — but not morbid — self-questioning. What makes us really tick? What are the things we live for? Do we need the constant support of achievement? Do we require the reassurance of approval for the things we do? Are we over concerned about appearance, clothes, etc.? Do we need the security money is supposed to bring? Do we long for a particular kind of housing? Are we dissatisfied with our present lot and do we often look wistfully over our shoulders to see if there is any new experience on the horizon which might bring us the satisfaction we have not yet found?

It is also necessary to think about the integrity of our personal Christian faith. Religious fervour sometimes gives rise to pride in spiritual achievements and sadly sometimes encourages an unhealthy spiritual superiority.

MAKING CONNECTIONS

In the silence we may well discover the useful art of 'making connections'. When a doctor is engaged in making a diagnosis he is looking for a series of related symptoms which, taken together, point to an understanding of the basic problem. He will enquire into your past health history and may even ask questions about your parents and grand-parents. As he does so his trained mind is 'making connections'.

Life is made up of a variety of events but our reaction to these events is not an isolated phenomenon. It depends upon the kind of people we are and how we have responded to similar related events in the past. It may also depend upon

14

our culture and our social environment. Our familiar responses can often be a fruitful source of reflective material. They may even reveal intolerance, bias, and a lack of appreciation of other points of view. As we become aware of these so we are more likely to respond to events helpfully. What a lot of misery is caused by people who will only examine one side of the coin; who see religious fervour as being acceptable when it is our kind of religion but subversive and dogmatic when it emanates from another source! To be aware of this is not necessarily to change our opinion overnight but it does make for greater understanding and a willingness to appreciate that true peace is not the absence of conflict but the ability to live in harmony with people with whom we disagree.

One of the healthy results of a growing ability to 'make connections' is the willingness to admit that we have been mistaken in our attitudes and that our actions have been based upon warped ideas. It is a false pride which will not allow a person to admit that they were in the wrong and now, in humility, want to put things right. It takes a really big person to be honest about failure. Little people have to stick to their positions because they cannot bear to own up to having made mistakes.

DEVELOPING OUR POTENTIAL

Growing self-awareness is not, however, a miserable process which only helps us to become aware of our inadequacies; it is also a means whereby we recognise the full value of ourselves as human beings who have much to give to others and who can find fulfilment in our own life experiences. Each moment can be lived so that it has meaning and significance. This does not mean an over-preoccupation with our own thought processes but it does mean that we are in touch with our own inner lives and so we can live much more healthily and fruitfully. Positive living is sometimes falsely portrayed as simply being an optimistic attitude towards life which always looks for the best and ignores the worst. Realistic living is a way of life which acknowledges within our own lives the darkness of sin and the light which comes from knowing that we are loved by God and lifted (saved) by our relationship with Jesus.

When we begin to love other people realistically we love them 'warts and all'. In marriage true love is not blind; it recognises the flaws and through deep sharing comes to terms with them. Out of such sharing there can emerge a new depth of relationship. It is this ability which can be given to us 'in the silence'. It is exciting to learn how we can benefit from reflecting on the nature of our relationships with others.

Our growth as persons is dependent entirely upon our ability to love, fully to appreciate our own worth and value and to utilise all our own gifts and talents. When that which lies within is healthy and alert then that which issues from it is fruitful and productive (see Mark 7:14–23).

JESUS POINTS THE WAY

We can benefit from examining the way Jesus dealt with the disciples. In so many ways they were a fickle band with all kinds of weaknesses and faults and failings. They were 'made' by his love for them and his acceptance of them just as they were. Sometimes he was stern with them: "Get behind me, Satan", he said to Peter who must have been deeply hurt by that incisive remark. Jesus discerned accurately what was going on inside them and knew that they would betray him and flee when the challenge came. But at the same time he saw their possibilities and helped them to develop their strengths and recognise their weaknesses. It was a hard way for all of them, involving pain and remorse, but he never ceased to love them and as they realised this more and more so their ability to respect themselves and love others grew and developed.

To become increasingly aware of ourselves is an important stepping stone to Christian maturity.

QUESTIONS FOR DISCUSSION

1. Do you recognise any part of yourself in the first section of this chapter? Share experiences and be ready to tell honestly if you feel that you do 'come alive' within the situations described. Can you think of ways in which inadequacy in child-parent relationships does spill over into our relationships with God and the Church? Give illustrations from your own life and the lives of others if they are relevant.

2. Detectives 'make connections' when they are trying to solve a crime and it is often out of those connections that a solution comes. Do you find 'making connections' between events in your life difficult or easy?

3. Explore the relationship Jesus had with his disciples. Did he help them to develop their awareness? If so, how? Look at incidents in the gospels and discuss what was actually going on between Jesus and his chosen band. Then see if those areas of understanding can become relevant in your own real life situations.

Seven daily readings about Awareness

ONE   **LIVING WITH SOLITUDE**

In all probability you are reading this in a room by yourself. You have chosen to be alone in order to reflect and pray. We all need to be alone from time to time. What are some of the advantages of solitude?

1. We can become more aware of ourselves and less likely to fall victim of self-delusion. You are quiet now. Slow down your breathing rate. Ask God to show you some aspect of yourself you need to know about.

2. We realise the importance of what we are as distinct from what we do. In society we are often judged by what we have achieved. In God's sight it is the quality of our inner lives and our outward loving and caring which matters most.

3. We become aware that God wants to give himself to us. If we are to share love we must first of all receive it from its original source.

Now read Matthew 4:1 – 11. This is what happened to Jesus when he want alone into the desert. His life was profoundly changed by this experience. If you chose to live part of your life in solitude what might this do for you?

TWO   **IMPROVING OUR VISION**

Read Mark 8:22 – 26
Note the varying stages of what happened to the blind man:
1. He was brought to Jesus by his friends.

2. They asked Jesus to help him.
3. Jesus touched his eyes.
4. He received partial vision.
5. Jesus touched his eyes again.
6. He could now see clearly.

Now say to yourself — I want to be able to see more clearly.
I want to be able to 'make connections' (see introductory
chapter on 'Awareness') and so make progress.

1. Come to God by yourself or with friends and ask for
   better vision.

2. Direct God's attention to an area of your life you would
   like to understand better.

3. Things have begun to happen. Insight has been given.

4. Ask God to enable you to see more clearly.

5. Feel his hands upon you. Your eyes are being opened.

6. As the vision clears be ready to obey its implications.

THREE   YOUR BODY LANGUAGE

Listen to what your body says to you. As you discover how
to read its signs so you are picking up information about
yourself.

Do you easily get tired? Then you are probably living with
an over-tensed body which needs to relax more.

Does your digestion go awry from time to time but usually
restore itself to order without recourse to doctors or
medicine? Then your nervous tension is expressing itself
through a particularly vulnerable part of you.

Do you suffer from frequent headaches? Then your anxiety

is being expressed through the nerves of the head which are particularly susceptible to the effects of strain.

Do you tend to overwork? This will also raise your tension levels and far from solving your problems will add to them.

Read 1 Corinthians 6:19−20

Are you using your body to God's glory — and thereby living a healthier life?

FOUR   MOMENTS OF TRUTH

Read Genesis 28:16 and recall the events which led to and from this important discovery.

Jacob had deceived his father through the subtlety of his mother and stolen from his brother Esau the parental blessing which was his rightful due. Esau was intent on killing his brother Jacob — the supplanter.

Jacob ran away into the most lonely place he could find. He wanted to escape from his brother, from his parents — and from God. He was afraid but he was also conscience-stricken. He realised the enormity of his sin.

It was for him a moment of truth. He had not expected to meet God in the wilderness but it was there that it happened.

Note the primitive and immature nature of Jacob's faith: "If God will be with me... then shall the Lord be my God". He was striking a bargain with God.

You cannot do that now any more than then, but it is still

true that there are 'moments of truth' when happenings outside of us and within us move towards a climax. In that moment we become sharply aware of who we truly are but also of what we might become.

Read on in Genesis 28 from verse 16 to verse 22.

What is your vow — pledge — promise — now that you are more aware of God's plan for your life?

FIVE   **FINDING FULFILMENT**

Most of us like to be liked. I know I do. Most of us are fond of success. I know I am. Such feelings are entirely normal. We need to be cherished and we need to be assured that we are useful people.

But there is a danger — and it is that we become so wedded to success that we live by it. The possibility of failure haunts us and if we think it has happened, we are cast down in despair. Experiences of rejection also bite deeply. We do so enjoy being wanted and accepted.

What sometimes happens is that when these danger signals begin to flash we strive harder to succeed and try more to be liked. There are, however, limits to our ability and from time to time we are bound to meet people who do not automatically take to us.

The answer lies in a realistic assessment of our potential and a wise acceptance of our limitations.

Jesus often turned human values upside down. *Read Luke 9:24.* In an understanding of this verse and attempting to put it into practice there is a real fulfilment.

Anxiety is wide-spread throughout society. In its advanced state it is a crippling neurosis which makes life seem hardly worth living. Those who are anxious at this level need help and guidance. But most of us suffer from bouts of anxiety about ourselves or those we love.

1. Try using creative thoughts to counter anxiety. *Read 2 Timothy 1:6 – 7.* Negative thoughts can be displaced by positive ones. Note especially the command to "stir into flame" *(Revised English Bible)* our original Christian experience. You can activate a counter-blast to anxiety by claiming God's promises and making them your own.

2. Remember that God is in ultimate control. *Read Psalm 46* and dwell upon its reassuring words. Take a sentence at a time and let each significant phrase 'soak in'. *Then read 1 Peter 5:7* but note also the following verse... "be on the alert" *(Revised English Bible).*

3. Cultivate the companionship of Jesus. His promise is in the last sentence of *Matthew's Gospel, 28:20.* God's gift of imagination can be a real source of help here. Visualise him stretching out his hand towards you and reaching the raw nerve of your anxiety.

Say out loud:

> *God in Jesus died for me, on the ridge of Calvary,*
> *God in Jesus rose for me, fair with immortality,*
> *God in Jesus lives for me, bearing with me patiently.*
> *(Anon.)*

Lord, I believe... help thou my unbelief.

STRENGTH THROUGH WEAKNESS

Our growing self-awareness requires that we recognise those areas of our lives where we are weak. In so doing we can actually develop our strengths.

I was born in Belper in Derbyshire. At one time a woman by the name of Phyliss Webber lived there. She spent her days in a wheelchair but on the wall of her stone house was a brass plate which read: *Derbyshire School of Speech and Drama*. She was its Principal. But it was an unusual school. Her students were mainly disturbed personalities who were sent to her by doctors. Under her guidance and inspiration they were helped to discover inward harmonies by expressing themselves in words and actions. She cast her own particular spell upon them. They saw how she had conquered. In her weakness lay her strength. In her disability lay her power to help others.

Julian of Norwich dwelt long on the wounds of Jesus. As she did so she became conscious of how our own wounds can be instruments of healing as his so evidently were. She sought from God the wound of loving compassion. This was undoubtedly given to her because she was able to help many people through her godly counsel and her gracious care. As she lingered with the wounds of Jesus so she absorbed his love for others and his desire to help them towards a greater wholeness.

Read Isaiah 53:1–5

When Paul wrote *1 Corinthians 1:25–28* was he thinking of his own 'strength through weakness' experience?

Julian of Norwich said that we should "know ourselves, what we are through him in nature and in grace". It was surely 'grace' that enabled Paul to grow through his weakness. It is reassuring to know that the thrust of life is with us and for us. Only so can our 'wounds' become our 'worships'.

(See *Julian of Norwich* by Grace Jantzen[1].)

2 CHANGE

"It's all change these days", said a weary church member to me a little while ago. "Why can't they leave things as they are? When the familiar guide-posts are gone I don't know where I am and I tend to get lost."

Ministers in pastoral charge of churches are often at the sharp end of this kind of remark and must always try to be sensitive to the needs of those who find their security threatened. But there is another aspect of pastoral experience which is the exact opposite. In every congregation there are also 'radicals' and 'progressives' who believe that the rate of change is too slow. They want to see far-reaching changes in liturgy, discipline and church order — and from time to time threaten to leave a church which seems to be dragging its feet so far as change is concerned.

In society generally there have been considerable changes in attitude towards a wide variety of social questions: abortion, homosexuality, conservation, the treatment of animals, the abuse of drugs and alcohol, to mention some of the most important and contentious. Because of this the respective churches have felt bound to re-examine all such matters and in recent years a spate of reports has been issued by the various denominations. They have differed sharply in their emphases and conclusions and often their publication has had an interesting effect. If a report has appeared too radical to some members of a particular church they have either set up a pressure group to oppose its adoption or established an unofficial working party to go over the same ground knowing that it would reach alternative conclusions. Equally if a report has come down on what seems to some to be the 'conservative' side then those who differ from its findings have done just the same thing — set up a pressure group or an unofficial working party.

This kind of dialogue can be healthy and life-giving providing those who participate respect the views of those who differ from them and grant them the right to hold those views. Often however there have been witch hunts and attempts to stifle both extreme conservatives and extreme radicals. This is seldom necessary unless some vital aspect of Christian truth is at stake. Often the act of exclusion brings a publicity to those concerned which is undesirable.

This chapter is not going to attack or support any particular change which has been suggested or has taken place in recent years. It sets out to deal with our attitudes to change and how we might be helped to think creatively about it. However, it is not without interest to note that changes in scientific and medical conclusions are usually easily accepted and described as progress whereas changes in liturgies and Christian social attitudes are thought to be in a different category. Is it perhaps because they are associated in people's minds with the fact of God who is believed to be changeless?

INTERNAL VALUES

Our social attitudes are related to our internal values and the kind of reasoning and thinking processes we have developed.

In his book entitled *Precarious Living*[2], Dr Martin Israel describes his own spiritual experience. Brought up in South Africa he experienced little direct love and affection from his professional parents who left him in the care of coloured servants whom he remembers with warm feelings and deep respect. Being 'brainy' he turned to intellectual pursuits but his emotional growth was stunted and when he came to England to continue medical studies he found personal relationships very difficult. He compensated by giving his entire attention to his work and studies and achieved a splendid academic record but even so did not find it easy to get jobs because of his extreme diffidence and shyness.

His release came through a helpful relationship with a 'stout, elderly woman' who taught psychology in evening

26

classes. Although familiar with the theories of Freud, Jung and Adler she was more concerned to help her pupils to discover themselves and to make progress in their own personal development. She spoke also of God and through this relationship his awareness that he was loved by God and could be a loving person was re-awakened. He became conscious of a keen, mystical streak which had in fact also characterised his earlier years and now felt quite sure that God was with him. Today he serves God through his work as a pathologist but also at the altar and in pastoral work as an ordained Anglican priest.

Dr Israel has changed from being nervous and withdrawn to someone who is now quietly confident of his own ability and the contribution he can make to other people's lives. What is more, he has been willing to expose the story of his pilgrimage in the book I have mentioned above, thereby helping many other people — including the one who writes these words!

Change then is going on all around us and change should be going on deep within us. Our physical bodies change as we grow older and unless we adjust and adapt as persons we shall not become the kind of mature people God wants us to be (see Ephesians 4:13–16).

ATTITUDES TO CHANGE

Our attitudes to change depend upon two essential factors: our thought life together with our reasoning powers — and our feelings. Both play a vital part in our development as persons and there needs to be a balance between them. Those whose decisions are all made cerebrally are in danger of becoming cold and impersonal; those whose activities are guided almost entirely by feelings are likely to be rash and irrational and to make serious mistakes. Here are three suggestions to help you to reflect upon your attitude towards change:

1. When you feel inwardly disturbed ask yourself the reason why.

All of us tend to react instinctively to people whose opinions we do not share and whose activities we resent. How often in the middle of some kind of political or industrial dispute when a particular person has been constantly interviewed on television you have exploded and said something like... "If that man (woman) comes on again I shall throw a hammer at the screen". Of course you don't really mean it. Television sets are far too expensive!

In another chapter I have written about 'bias'; we have seen that we have a predisposition to 'lean' in a certain direction. This is natural. Like a computer we have been 'programmed' by our past experience and when certain events take place we respond in a predictable way.

The habit of stopping to think why we do so respond can have many useful effects. It can make us question the normal responses of being a person from a certain kind of cultural background. People who live in a particular kind of area often read the same newspapers and hold similar political and social views. We reflect our environment and our social status. This is reasonable but it is necessary for it to be questioned from time to time. Am I being something of a cipher on this particular issue? Is there another side to this argument which I should be hearing? Do I always have to reflect the views and indeed the actions of the people I seem to relate to most naturally?

2. What are the gospel insights on this particular matter?

This is particularly important. I have sometimes been shaken by the views on racial matters of some people I know, love and respect. What to me is quite clear from the gospel — that all men and women are equal and have the right to be treated as such — does not always seem to be so clear to others. I certainly do not set myself up as a judge.

On other issues it is likely that gospel insights have not sharpened my own views. But it is surely axiomatic that if we have chosen to live by the good news of the gospel of Jesus we cannot be selective about what we will accept and what we will reject.

3. Bring 'feelings' and 'gospel insights' together in reflective prayer.

I must now write out of personal experience. When I do this a number of things happen to me. First of all I touch a deeper stratum of reality within myself. If I have been disappointed and sorry for myself and perhaps even bitter about something, this kind of reflection has often shown me that the reason for it lies in my own inadequacy. I needed something to bolster me up as a person. I did not find it and so have felt rejected. The answer lies not within further striving to achieve but in acceptance and in the learning process which can take place. In this respect I have been helped to change — and I believe changed for the better.

Secondly, I am helped in my attitude towards other people. Things that happen in life are often due to the judgements and actions of others. If things have turned out well for me then I am benevolently disposed towards them; if not, I am tempted to dislike them and even work against them. Prayerful reflection has given me a calmer and more balanced view and moved me to try to relate helpfully towards the people concerned. A number of very useful relationships in my life have emerged out of quite negative feelings.

Thirdly — and most importantly, I am helped to see something of 'the mind of Christ'. This awareness of being on his wavelength is a tremendous spur and has from time to time brought about internal and external changes in my life.

JESUS AND CHANGE

Jesus was sensitive both to people and social situations. He did not allow others to mould him or else he would have been the popular leader of a revolutionary movement. He recognised different kinds of needs. He could be sharp with people he believed were play-acting (the Pharisees), and warm and caring with people who had sinned but who were aware of it (Mary Magdalene, Zaccheus, Matthew). He saw many people change dramatically (Peter, Thomas, Paul — "one born out of due time"). Down the years he has gone on bringing meaning and purpose to people's lives and providing the dynamic to escape from one's 'breeding' or 'grooming' or 'deprivation' or 'emotional insecurity' — and to such he has given life and hope.

We live in an age of change. Only changed and changing lives can meet its challenge.

QUESTIONS FOR DISCUSSION

1. Recall some of the changes which have taken place in the shape of the liturgy and in Christian social attitudes in recent years. (List a few of them on a wall sheet.) What has your attitude been towards them? Are you pleased that changes have come or do you long for the more tranquil days when the pace of life was slower?

2. Discuss the ways in which attitudes towards change are determined. Consider the part played by feelings in making decisions and the part played by one's reasoning powers. How can we make sure that both aspects of our humanity play their proper part in determining our attitudes towards change?

3. Is it possible to be a responsible person and live for a long time without being sure which side is right in an area of deep division? Name such an issue where to make up your mind has proved extremely difficult.

Seven daily readings about Change

ONE   **CONVERSION**

Read the Saul/Paul drama in Acts 9:1–22.

Note the progressive stages of Paul's 'change' experience: inward unrest which prompted him to persecute the Christians even more; the supreme moment of insight on the Damascus Road; the need for time to reflect upon what had happened — this made possible by his temporary blindness: a visit from a new friend, Ananias, who touched him lovingly and called him 'brother'; now he goes straight to the synagogue and proclaims the Lordship of Jesus! Some of the disciples are suspicious and will not accept him but again a friend stands by him and becomes his guarantor. Now he is really in business as an apostle.

Perhaps only parts of this experience have — or will — come our way. Think about some of them and identify them in your mind: unrest — a state of mind which often precedes healthy change; dissatisfaction with ourselves as we are; challenge through a friend, a book or a feeling from deep within ourselves which rises up in a time of quiet; the touch of someone's hand and their kindly interest in our well-being; action of some kind which may result in misunderstanding.

Conversions/changes are not just 'once for all' experiences; they can and indeed should go on happening throughout our lives. If we avoid change, we may also avoid growth.

God is not a good habit,
a useful Sunday exercise,
one interest among others,
a fascinating hobby,
a crutch in times of need.

God is life itself;
he is Someone —
not to be analysed,
examined, proved —
but to be met.

And when it happens
life unfolds,
meanings matter,
love is deeper,
quality counts.

Be still.
Relax,
Unwind.
Open those inner doors.

Resurgam! *I shall arise!*

Read :Corinthians 5:16–21. Demonstrate verse 17 in your life today!

THREE   **NEW BEGINNINGS**

Read Psalm 51

From time to time in life things happen to us which cause us to feel in need of forgiveness. Now to be forgiven is not a negative experience which simply wipes out the mistakes we have made. It is — or should be — a positive, learning experience, which enables us to move forward into a new quality of living.

Note verse 3. It is always good to be specific. Asking for forgiveness in a general way is of little use. Herein lies the value of confession whether it be in a formal or informal setting. To 'recognise' that which lies at the heart of a particular aspect of failure makes good sense.

Now re-read verses 16 and 17. The idea of trying to deserve forgiveness is 'out'. Nothing we can do can merit God's favour. The basic requirement is total sincerity.

Finally go back to verse 10. Our new and different behaviour in the area of our wrongdoing will arise out of what God does for us in response to our cry for help.

Real changes take place deep inside our inner beings. They then result in new kinds of action. Put your own life inside this Psalm. You have read the Psalm: let the Psalm read you.

FOUR   **THE WELL OF NEED**

A friend of mine who died recently wrote an article with the above title. It was based on the familiar story of the woman of Samaria. *Read John 4:1 – 30.*

He had himself passed through deep emotional traumas and saw within this story a parable of life.

The woman wanted to be loved. She had moved from one

relationship to another in search of fulfilment but she had not found it. What was wrong?

She had, in all probability, never recognised her own real need. She had never been herself. She had worn a mask; tried to be what she thought men wanted her to be — attractive and pliable. But it hadn't worked.

It never does. The gospel truth is that you are loved just as you are. You don't have to put on a show; you don't have to act out a part. Be yourself and find a group of people who will accept you just as you are. Then you are on the road to a new life.

My friend concluded his article with this phrase which has burnt itself into my memory: "His love will never let us go, never let us down, and, in all honesty, never let us off!"

Have you noticed the relationship between today's reading and yesterday's?

FIVE   CONFORM OR BE TRANSFORMED

Sometimes a verse from a less familiar version of the Bible stabs you awake. J. B. Phillips did this for me years ago with his translation of Romans 12:2: "Don't let the world around you squeeze you into its own mould but let God re-mould your lives from within..."

Now read the immediate context in Romans 12:1-2

In my experience followers of Jesus tend to hold similar opinions to those of the majority of the people around them, shown in the kind of newspapers they read; the political party they vote for; the views they hold on matters of social concern. The pressures upon us to conform are very strong.

This is also true of our opinions about international relations. The media tell us that certain nations are to be feared and others are to be trusted. If ever we get to know individuals who belong to a 'feared' nation, we often discover that they are just human beings like ourselves with the same hopes and aspirations.

If there was greater understanding between religions and races and nations there would be less fear and anxiety.

Change has to begin somewhere. Why not within you? Read the passage again and ponder.

SIX   LOVE IN ACTION

I was once responsible for a training/fellowship week for ministerial colleagues. Naturally I wanted it to go well and worked hard at my preparation and all the administrative chores. But when the week was in progress my anxiety showed through. One of the brethren challenged me about it and said to me plainly:
"Howard, we want you to know that we love you!"

It was as if something broke inside me. The inner tension and the fierce desire for the week to be a success vanished. Later on I asked them all to lay their hands upon me in blessing. They did and it helped me even more.

This is how real changes take place. When you realise that you are loved and you feel a deep inner urge to love in response. Doors are opened inside yourself and into other people's lives.

Now read 1 John 4:7−21

I am loved... I can love... I must go on loving. Praise God!

Look back at section four. Evidently I have something in common with the woman at Sychar. Have you?

SEVEN   NEW FOR OLD

I always have to read George Herbert's poems at least three times — and slowly — to get the meaning out of them.

> *Who would have thought my shrivell'd heart*
> *Could have recovered greenness? It was gone*
> *Quite underground, as flowers depart*
> *To feed their mother-root when they have blown;*
> *Where they together*
> *All the hard weather,*
> *Dead to the world, keep house unknown.*
>
> *These are thy wonders, Lord of Power,*
> *Killing and quick'ning, bringing down to hell*
> *And up to heaven in an hour;*
> *Making a chiming of a passing bell.*
> *We say amiss,*
> *This or that is:*
> *Thy word is all, if we could spell.*

Read John 12:24 and Galatians 2:20

The experiences outlined in both poem and scripture are possible for ordinary people. Within the old — that which has passed and is passing — there is the seed of a new life. From what has gone you can discover what may be.

3 INVASION

The title of this booklet implies a steady movement towards maturity with continuing growth being at the heart and centre of the experience. This chapter, however, suggests that within that growth experience there are — or can be — times when life moves much more quickly in a positive and energising direction. Internal and external pressures operating at the same time seem to be making available a power which can take us on to a new stage in life. Sometimes the greater 'push' seems to come from within ourselves and sometimes it seems to come from outside sources.

While this was being written I had a visit from a man who felt that he wanted to share with me an experience which had come to him some few years before. He described how low he had felt and how near he was to breaking down. Then he said... "It was as though I was taken hold of... worship experiences began to mean much more to me... I began to see myself as I really was but at the same time I became aware that I need not remain in that state... I was lifted up to a new level of experience and it has held me ever since".

I have talked to many people who have been affected by the various kinds of renewal movements which are touching the life of the whole Church right across the world. Those who have been blessed by 'charismatic' renewal have told me how they became liberated. Once they were in slavery to what other people thought of them; they had to be successful and to be seen to have the trappings of success. One told me of an entirely new ability to be thankful and to really praise God for the ordinary blessings of life.

Another time I was in the company of two people — one elderly and one young — who had both come into new and transforming experiences arising out of their discovery of new ways of praying. It was fascinating to hear how two people of such different ages and from such different backgrounds had come to share this common blessing. They just wanted to say together in the words of an old hymn: "From shades of night to plains of light, O praise his name, he lifted me".

FOCUS ON CONTEMPORARY WRITERS

A different kind of insight comes from a group of authors who have discerned within the pattern of today's world events the possibility of "an evolutionary leap forward in the realm of the Spirit". Stephen Verney in his book *Into the New Age*[3] sees two possibilities before mankind: the one awesome and terrible because it contains within it the possibility of destruction and annihilation; the other still awesome but full of hope because it will usher in a new depth of spiritual experience. This new depth will mean... "that we become more aware of ourselves, more responsible to each other and more willing to co-operate with the creative centre of divine love" (page 33).

Canon Peter Spink takes up the same theme in a book which he calls *Spiritual Man in a New Age*[4]. He believes that both inside and outside the Church there is a new movement towards 'interior awareness'. This movement when firmly anchored in Jesus gives rise to a new and deeper sense of Christ-consciousness: "It is this belief that there is a potential in man beyond ordinary living, a dimension of a new humanity which is the factor common to those who today are involved in the search and to those who are recognised as throwing light on the path" (page 37). The Omega Order which he has founded aims, among other things: "to follow those spiritual disciplines which awaken the heart to the truth as it is in Jesus".

Roger Grainger, a hospital chaplain in a large mental hospital, in his book *Watching for Wings*[5] points out the need to appreciate the importance of divine intervention in any kind of healing process. While accepting all that is best in physical, surgical and psychological medicine, he insists that another factor be taken seriously. That is the Christ factor: "Only through 'third-person' therapy can the weakness which cries out to be strengthened become the maturity that knows the nature of real strength; not something appropriated, something grasped, but a gift given and received" (page 77).

Gerald O'Collins has written a book about "spiritual awareness and the mid-life crisis" which he calls *The Second Journey*[6]. He begins by telling the stories of some outstanding people who have 'begun again' in life's midstream: Malcolm Muggeridge, John Wesley, President Jimmy Carter, Cardinal Newman, are all offered as illustrations. The new possibilities begin to make themselves clear but the price of a new awakening is sometimes high: "We must let go if we are to be broken up, remade and restructured. Our world suddenly comes apart at the seams. We cannot mend it. Let it come apart — even at the cost of much pain. But out of that coming apart there is 'new birth'. We have to 'die' in order that we may 'live'."

All these authors have one thing in common — they believe that a divine initiative is very much part of the present scene. God is active in his own world and in the hearts and lives of people of different traditions and religions. We are the fortunate witnesses of a divine invasion — more that that, we are potential beneficiaries!

THE BIBLICAL BASIS

What better word is there to describe this act of God intervening in human lives and communities than the New Testament word 'grace'?

The constant emphasis in the Bible is that God is always taking the initiative in bringing home the possibility of men and women sharing in the salvation event. In the Old

Testament God's 'loving-kindness' lies at the heart of the covenant relationship. This depends more upon God's love than upon man's response, although man's response is the proper consequence of becoming aware of God's love.

Paul was quite sure that God's choice of Israel was the direct outcome of his 'grace'. Similarly the Christian life itself is God's 'free gift' (Ephesians 2:4−9) and is not the outcome of man's deserving (2 Tim. 1:9). Paul even suggests that man's response is only possible because of "grace" (Ephesians 1:19; Phil. 1:29). Paul's experience, however, indicated that man's response was required but he just wanted to emphasise that it was "all of grace". Perhaps the text which best expresses Paul's sense of indebtedness to God combined with the need to make the best use of what you are given is Philippians 2:12ff: "Work out your own salvation with fear and trembling; for it is God which worketh in you both to will and to do his good pleasure."

The direct consequence of our awareness that we are the fortunate recipients of God's grace is, hopefully, that we make the best possible use of it in our development as persons and as Christian disciples. We must make the most of these peak periods of our lives when we become directly aware that God is making effective contact with us.

CULTIVATING A TRUSTING ATTITUDE

The idea that we have to "earn our passage" dies hard. We are surrounded by people who believe that "you get what you work for" and we can very easily carry this philosophy over into the realm of religion. From time to time we need to remind ourselves that a trustful attitude towards life can eliminate much destructive anxiety.

A woman I know received a deep disappointment. She had hoped for a particular place in life which was denied her. Humanly speaking she had to settle for what, on the surface, seemed much less. She resented it deeply and was desperately unhappy. Then one day God spoke to her apparently without any human intermediary. She realised that her misery was largely self-inflicted. Within her situation there were tremendous possibilities which she had failed to see because of her bitterness. She woke up one day with a completely new attitude. The circumstances hadn't changed but she had. She now began to affirm life rather than deny it. In the end the job she had gave her satisfaction and contentment. Her one regret was the time wasted in self-pity after her great disappointment. The new quality in her life was that of trust and she was quite sure that behind this sudden and dramatic transformation was the grace of God.

Her experience indicates that we should all...

MAKE THE MOST OF LIFE'S CREATIVE MOMENTS

Some people have not become part of the evolutionary 'leap forward' because they have not responded to God's moment.

Many years ago I used to notice a small lady creep into the back row of my church and then slip out again before anyone could get to speak to her. One day I managed to reach her at the church gateway and invited myself to her home. There I met her daughter who was a Down's Syndrome child and the mother told me the story of how her birth had changed their lives. Prior to the birth she and her husband were a happy couple, deeply involved in a local church and looking forward to the birth of their first child. When they discovered she suffered from Down's Syndrome they left their church and withdrew from all forms of social contact, only going out for work and shopping. They felt that the child must be a punishment for some sin they had committed although they did not know what it could have been. But for some time she felt that God had been speaking to her and telling her to get back to church. She came to mine because she was not known there but had tried to avoid all forms of personal contact. She had kept this up for months until I managed to make contact with her.

Our meeting turned out to be God's moment for her. Once the whole matter was out in the open and she began to meet with other people with the same kind of problem, life took on a new meaning. The first thing she discovered was that her daughter was the most lovable child in the world! She and her husband came right back into the life of the church and began to help the local mentally-handicapped association. I should emphasise that this was thirty years ago when social attitudes to all forms of mental handicap were far different from those of today.

God got through to them. He had tried a number of times and had been repelled — but at last "they came to themselves" and so began a new and developing chapter in their lives. Once they had responded there were many new and exciting experiences in store for them.

Be ready for God's moments. Just as Jesus came "in fullness of time" so there are occasions in all our lives when the circumstances are just right for God to enter our lives in a new way. If we are fearful because we feel that there is a risk involved, just hold up the possibilities and the risk quietly before God and he will show you just what the positive prospects are. God is always preparing the way for some new invasion of our lives. His grace guarantees it. He will also help us to respond if we ask him!

QUESTIONS FOR DISCUSSION

1. Does this idea of there being special moments when God draws near in special ways ring true with your experience? Go round the group and say whether you can recall times when this was so. Can you recall any of God's moments which you did not respond to and regretted it afterwards?

2. This chapter refers to a book entitled *The Second Journey*, which suggests that middle life (whenever that is — say between 40 and 60) often offers the opportunity for a completely new start in life. Why should this be so? What are the factors which make this a more real possibility than say at a much earlier and a much later stage?

3. Look up some of the Bible references to 'grace' given in this chapter. In what way would you define 'grace'? Was Pentecost an occasion for a special outpouring of 'grace'? Do the biblical and psychological concepts of growth agree or had the Bible a special offer to make which goes beyond psychological theories and explanations of human growth?

Seven daily readings about Invasion

ONE   READY TO RECEIVE

In recent years I have come to see how important it is to try to provide genuine spiritual experiences for those who are being prepared for confirmation. Previously I had placed great emphasis upon clear and precise instruction in the Christian Faith. This is still necessary although it is best if young people can be stimulated to ask their own questions.

I have taken them to a religious community and helped them to get the 'feel' of the place. I have tried to communicate the essential 'spirit' of the house as it has taken hold of me. In the chapel I have invited them to be quiet and to let the love and light and power of God flow around them.

Then I have taken them to a geriatric hospital so that they can also get the 'feel' of helplessness and deep human need.

In conversations afterwards they have referred to the importance of these events. Both in the silence and in the deep human need they have 'felt' the presence and power of God.

Read Job 42:1 – 6. Recall Job's problems. Why do innocent people suffer? Why have such terrible things happened to me? He gets no complete and final answers to his difficulties. Instead he sees God (verse 5). This makes all the difference. It still does!

TWO   GRACE ABOUNDING

Read Acts 3:1 – 10

1. The man in need had to ask for help. He was entirely dependent on the generosity of other people and just managed to survive.

2. On this day he got more than he asked for: no money but a cure for his illness. Whereas he had been so crippled that he could not walk, now he was able to stand up.

3. He immediately exercised his restored limbs. He 'jumped' up and walked around.

4. He praised God. He did not attribute the healing to Peter and John although he was grateful for the part they had played. He recognised that they were God's servants and that God's grace had marvellously affected his whole being.

So...

44

1. Don't be afraid to ask for help in a direct area of your life.

2. Be prepared that the answer sometimes comes in an unexpected way.

3. When something happens to you, act upon it. Exercise the restored faculty.

4. Give thanks and praise to God. He has 'invaded' your life.

THREE   ALIVE WITH HIS LIFE

Read Ephesians 2:4 – 10

Note all the positive assertions in this passage and underline them in your Bible: "he brought us to life", "he raised us up"; "he has created us for a life of good works"; and others in a similar vein. If you put down in one column the references to what God has done and then in another column the references to man's response you will see how much longer one is than the other and so where the emphasis lies.

There are two key words in the passage — grace and faith.

Grace. The first definition of the word 'grace' I ever heard was that it is God's love in action. I have never been able to improve upon it.

Faith. Not an intellectual assent but a quiet trust that God is on your side and is working in your best interests even when, on the surface, this seems far from the truth.

It is a profound moment when you realise that God is seeking you. He wants to live and move in you. His delicate hand would open you up so that you may flower in his sunshine.

Trust him — even though your trust be small — and you will begin to come alive!

FOUR   SUDDENLY IT HAPPENED

C. S. Lewis and Monica Furlong are two people who, in different ways, speak to this generation. Their Christian experience seems to be authentic and mature. What they write seems to "ring a bell" in many people's hearts and lives.

They each tell of special moments when "suddenly it happened". C. S. Lewis was going up Headington Hill on the top of a bus: "I became aware that I was holding something at bay or shutting something out... I chose to open, to unbuckle, to unloose the rein". In that moment of perception he "thawed out" and became different.

Monica Furlong was sitting on a bench in London Park at the age of twenty. She had "a shattering vision of joy and goodness and went away aghast at what had happened to me".

"Suddenly it happened" to a prison warder *as we read in Acts 16:25 – 34.*

In this story there was a crisis (an earthquake) and two human agents (Paul and Silas). There often is — although it is not necessarily so. God acts. He invades human lives in a variety of special ways. Many of us can look back to a moment of perception when "suddenly it happened".

Recall such moments and be thankful!

You must have heard it said many times and you have also said it about yourself: "Sorry, but this is the way I am... I was made like this... you must take me or leave me. I can't change".

You are right to accept that there is a powerful pull within you which is programmed against change. As we saw in the chapter on 'Awareness', personality traits are laid down early and they are with us all our days.

But this does not mean that change is impossible. If it were so then the gospel would not be 'good news', which it is — good news about the possibility of change!

Now I know my own heart, so, on the basis of this knowledge, I know that you, the reader, have let God down from time to time. You have failed to live up to what you have professed.

We all know that this experience was shared by the disciple, Peter. Now read *John 21:15–19*. The next stage is to imagine yourself in Peter's place. The conversation is taking place between you and Jesus. Go on! Imagination is one of God's gifts — use it!

The Lord has a special work for *you* — and only *you* can do it.

When you know what it is — be it large or small, immediate or long-term — read and obey that final phrase: "Follow me!"

People who telephone me often begin by saying, "I'm sorry to bother you because I know how busy you are". Sometimes I let it go although from time to time I do insist that I am available and ready to give time to whatever they need. I sometimes wonder how they would react if I said, "No, I'm not too busy; I'm free today, tomorrow and the whole week". They might think that "if he has so much free time he can't have much to offer" and not bother to ring me again.

Being busy has become part of our lifestyle. If we have an empty space we fill it. We ring up a friend for a chat; we go to where there are people in the hope that we shall meet someone. When we are alone we tend to switch on the radio or TV so that the silence will not overwhelm us.

What a waste of time! How foolish it is to avoid the silence. It provides just the opportunity God needs. He wants you to be quiet for some part of every day so that he can get through to you. He needs to know that your number is absolutely free so that he can dial you and make contact.

Recall what happened to Elijah by *reading 1 Kings 19:9–18*. God had a message to give him but Elijah was suffering from post-victory depression. He had been exalted by success. Now he was fearful of what might be the consequence.

God reached him through the silence and gave him his marching orders.

Listen now — and often — for the "soft whisper of a voice". Give him space. Let him come in!

I was doing a 'one-off' in the Young People's Fellowship one Sunday afternoon. I put a question up on the flip-chart and invited immediate discussion about it. The question was: "What makes life worth living?" Between us we hammered out three answers which we put up on the chart underneath the question. They were:

1. *Being loved and wanted and feeling to be a person of worth.*
2. *Being accepted in society; able to form relationships.*
3. *Having a satisfying job which pays enough to be able to live comfortably.*

I then asked the question: "Is that what we mean by Christian discipleship?" Most of them thought that there must be something more so I suggested that we looked at *1 John 3:13–20*. Will you take a look at it too, please?

We talked a good deal around the verse (14) which tells us about passing over from death to life. Pretty strong language this and we queried if we could take it seriously. It also has a lot to say about love. One of them came up with a verse from a pop song:

> *Say, can you love when you're hurt, brother?*
> *Or when you're rubbed in the dirt, brother?*
> *If not, its got to be said —*
> *You're dead!*

We decided that we couldn't go into that kind of 'over-drive' in our own strength. We needed some kind of outside invasion to get us started. Then we thought around the idea of resurrection and asked how the Easter message applied to us individually.

The verse we took home was *2 Corinthians 4:14*. The experience described there was (and is) our only hope of ever getting into over-drive.

4 PROBLEMS

Although now officially retired, I often meet people with problems. Sometimes they are relatively simple and cause no great distress. Often, however, they are complex and difficult and cause a great deal of pain and suffering.

In our society there are many organisations which have been founded to help people with their problems: Samaritans, Alcoholics Anonymous (and all the other 'anonymous' organisations which follow the same pattern), Citizen's Advice Bureaux, Marriage Guidance (and many other counselling organisations). Almost every serious illness has an organisation to help those who suffer from it: epilepsy, arthritis, multiple sclerosis — and dozens more. There are groups for the bereaved, the widowed, for childless couples and so on. Every natural grouping of problems seems to have an organisation to help people who fall into their particular category.

The facing of problems is a natural part of living. Those people who find the normal, everyday experience of life too much for them have indeed got problems! From the earliest days of our lives we are called upon to endure pain and make choices. "Man was made for joy and woe", said William Blake. There can be no real growth without our developing an ability to face and deal with the problems life inevitably brings. Perhaps the first step is to try to see (although sometimes it will be extremely difficult) that within every problem situation there is an opportunity.

The lovely prayer written by the theologian Reinhold Niebuhr has been repeated again and again. I have seen it hanging on study walls, on desks and in some rooms used for counselling: "God, grant me the serenity to accept the things I cannot change, courage to change the things I can, and the wisdom to know the difference".

It makes a good starting point for our discussion about

seeing the problems which life brings as potential "stepping stones to maturity".

ACCEPTANCE

Acceptance is often thought of in a negative way as being dull resignation. "What is to be will be". Sometimes the words of Jesus are quoted in support of this view: "Nevertheless not my will but thine be done". But the acceptance Jesus demonstrated was not dull resignation; it was an honest facing of reality out of which there came freedom and liberation. The cross which Jesus accepted has become the symbol of victory. Those who put him there were vanquished and "by his stripes we are healed". When Jesus "steadfastly set his face to go towards Jerusalem", he knew that this was what he had to do — and that out of his sacrifice new life and hope would come to many people. It did and it does!

Early in my pastoral experience I was present at the actual moment when a blind housewife was deserted by her husband for another woman. Apologetically he told her again that he was sorry, said a faltering goodbye, picked up his case and walked out through the door never to return. I expected that she would collapse. Not so. "Well", she said, "Now I have to begin a new life!" She did and made a wonderful job of it. In some ways her own personality was enlarged because whereas previously she had relied upon her husband for so many things, now she had to make decisions herself and assume full responsibility for the home. I hope I don't give the impression that there was no sadness! On the contrary there was very real grief and a deep fear of loneliness, but it was not allowed to swamp her. She sought help and support from others and she asked God to give her courage. He did.

One service I tried to provide in those circumstances was to help her see the reality of the situation which she faced and this can lead us naturally to another important point about tackling our problems.

SEE SITUATIONS AS THEY REALLY ARE

Most of us at one time or another in our lives make mountains out of molehills. We lose our sense of proportion about a situation and we worry so much that the effect it has upon us is out of balance with the nature of the problem itself.

A useful habit is to write a description of the situation on paper with the positive and negative aspects set out side by side. Sometimes this simple act serves to cut an issue down to its proper size. Sharing the problem with someone you trust is another way of finding help in making an accurate assessment. A wise friend will allow us to use him as a sounding board. He will neither belittle nor exaggerate the problem but will help us to see it as it really is.

Retreating from problems in the hope that they will go away is not to be recommended but facing situations openly and honestly sometimes means that we discover that we don't have a real problem after all! Many of the illnesses which take patients into their GP's surgeries actually resolve themselves without direct medical intervention other than the consultation. Some observers put the figure as high as 50 per cent. The body possesses its own natural healing powers which cope with many of the health problems which arise.

A wise doctor can often help us to learn from our illness symptoms. Sometimes we are displaying in our bodies our inadequacies as persons. When we are helped forward into more positive ways of living then some symptoms just disappear. This is also true of many of our anxieties. They arise more out of what we are than out of our circumstances. The change required is an inner change.

All this points to the importance of reflective prayer and the seeking for inner quiet. When we have discovered an inner reservoir of peace we can see problems much more clearly and also discover the strength to do something about them.

RECOGNISE THE STRENGTH OF YOUR FEELINGS

Long before we became capable of reflective thought we experienced a variety of feelings. We knew what it was to feel rejected by our parents and perhaps we were made to feel 'bad inside' by strong disapproval. We then discovered how to 'manipulate' those people set in authority over us and tried to avoid pain by securing their favour.

Later we may have longed for love and acceptance and found it hard to come by. This longing can become part of our inner psyche and is repeated again and again in our adult experience. Strong feelings thus cause anxiety and we tend to respond to situations in childish ways and cause ourselves a great deal of unhappiness. Developing the ability to recognise what is happening to us is an asset we have already discussed in the chapter on 'Awareness' but it also relates directly to the way we tackle problems. Our feelings can often override our reasoning and reflective abilities and this can lead to irrational and unwise decision-making which compounds rather than solves our problems.

EXPRESS YOUR FEELINGS

There is a wide-spread myth that decent people — and particularly Christians — should never be angry. A little thought soon indicates how false a view this is. Many of the social reforms that have taken place in our society happened because there were those who became very angry with what they observed. Anger is a natural emotion in the mature person and needs to be expressed.

Dylan Thomas wrote some famous lines as his father lay dying:

Do not go gentle into that good night.
Old age should burn and rage at close of day;
Rage, rage against the dying of the light.

Just as Dylan Thomas urged his father to 'rage' against his own dying so too we should sometimes 'rage' at death. Especially is this so when someone we love dies prematurely. Our anger should be allowed to mingle with our grief. We should express what we feel even if, on later reflection, it sounds blasphemous. God understands. Better to let our feelings go than to put a tight lid on them and "batten down the hatches". The eruption will come sooner or later. Far better that the feelings should be expressed in conjunction with the event. If they are allowed to smoulder deep inside us then one day strange things may begin to happen which only expert help will enable us to relate to our unexpressed grief and our suppressed anger. Prevention is better than cure.

Within a marriage relationship it is useful to have the contractual arrangement which agrees that feelings can be expressed without there being failure in loving. Often a build-up of small things can threaten a marriage. Destructive anger which means to hurt will harm the relationship. Controlled anger which expresses itself carefully but definitely can be healing and cleansing in its effects.

When The Prophet, Kahlil Gibran, was asked to speak of friendship he replied:

"When your friend speaks his mind you fear not the 'nay' in your own mind nor do you withhold the 'ay'."

Love is capable of absorbing what we feel about each other and can become much more real in the process. It thrives on honesty and not on a studied form of deception which avoids real meeting by shutting out anger.

Problems then are the raw material of living. In facing them we can find ourselves at a deeper level and can enjoy meeting other people in depth as well. Most of the difficulties we face in life contain within them the means whereby we may move forward into new areas of understanding.

I have known two men in senior jobs in the business world who had to face a similar problem. It was how to remain true to their faith and beliefs and be party to practices they did not believe in. Both took a firm stand. One lost his job; the other kept it. But both men retained their integrity and, as they told me afterwards, things happened to them during those difficult days which gave them strength and insights for the rest of their lives.

Problems can be opportunities in disguise.

QUESTIONS FOR DISCUSSION

1. Share experiences. Let members of the group describe a particular problem situation they have faced. Be prepared to speak of the negative and positive aspects of the incidents as you recall them. Are there some situations in life when to speak of a problem as an opportunity is blasphemy? If you think so — say so.

2. Discuss the following: "Suffering offers a detachment and a transcendence. It makes all our material possessions seem so unimportant and frees us to go beyond them and find the real value of living".

3. Here are two typical 'Americanisms': "Don't sweat the small stuff" and "If you must worry save it for the big occasion". Do we tend to magnify our problems and make them much bigger than they are?

Seven daily readings about Problems

ONE   BETRAYED

Read Psalm 55

A man had a friend. He trusted in him, confided in him, loved him (verses 13 and 14). But the friend let him down. The outcome of this act of betrayal was a deep and sensitive agonising.

Note the realism in the Psalm. The author's feelings have been profoundly affected. He is bitter and wants the wrong to be avenged. When you feel something deeply, *express it*. As we say in the introductory article on 'Problems', there are real dangers in burying what we really feel. You may even think that what you are saying out loud is totally lacking in forgiveness. Never mind. God understands. "He knows our frame".

The aggrieved party in the Psalm wants action. He wants the offender to be punished and would like to be there when it happens. He need not have worried. The man who had betrayed him had also betrayed himself. He had cut himself down in size. He may have seemed to be "riding on the crest of a wave" but he had actually damaged his own inner being. This would inevitably catch up with him unless he acknowledged his sin and failure and sought forgiveness.

Take verse 22 as your guide. Problems of relationships are often complex and difficult but they can be improved by putting them in God's hands. Sometimes this will mean a solution. Sometimes we shall be given the ability to cope with them without much obvious improvement.

Are realism, anger and trust called for in any situation with which you are involved? If not now, remember Psalm 55 — you are bound to need it someday!

TWO   LONELINESS

Is loneliness a problem? For many people it is. Suddenly they are bereaved. After a lifetime of companionship they are left alone. No head lies beside theirs on the pillow. No one is there with whom we can discuss the details of everyday existence. Others have longed for warm and intimate relationships but they have never come their way. When they seem to be developing, sometimes they become threatening and so they withdraw.

Perhaps we need to experience loneliness in our lives. Perhaps we need to face the agony of feeling isolated and misunderstood in order to realise our own true identity. Henri Nouwen expresses it in this way: "...the wound of loneliness is... a deep incision in the surface of our existence... which can be an inexhaustible source of beauty and self-understanding".

Those who have faced a deep, personal tragedy have told me: "I had to go away by myself and work it out. Other people helped me but there was a point at which I had to tackle it alone".

We need to cultivate loneliness so that when physical loneliness comes we are prepared.

Read Matthew 11:28−30. These verses are his promise to you. They will come alive in your loneliness. Think about Simone Weil's words also: "Waiting patiently in expectation is the foundation of spiritual life".

People who go to church and call themselves Christians are supposed to pray — but many don't. Some who do find it more of a burden than a delight. They pray spasmodically — often because they feel guilty about not praying.

Yet the basic elements in prayer are present in the raw material of our daily living. Those peak moments of existence we can recall — what were they all about?

Praise? Think of a time when spontaneous thanksgiving rose from deep inside you. A child is born. A friendship upholds you. A response to your loving becomes evident. Yes, you are praising, you are giving thanks.

Contemplation? You are on top of a high mountain looking down on a winding road. You are by a lakeside and reminded of depth. You are reading a poem or looking at a picture. Your mind becomes still and you are in the grip of a totally enjoyable experience.

Confession? You feel bad about something you have done. It all happened so quickly. You didn't mean to hurt — but you did. Now you are totally and utterly sorry.

These are all real life experiences. Prayer gives them an added depth and a deeper meaning.

Read Luke 11:1 – 13. It is all here: God, food, sin, persistence, fathers and sons... essential aspects of real life. Prayer of this kind makes life more demanding — but much more interesting!

Mother Julian is now annually commemorated as a saint on the 8th of May. In 1373 she received a series of sixteen 'shewings' of our Lord. She then became an 'anchoress', that is a woman dedicated to religion, and lived alone in a cell attached to St Julian's Church in Norwich.

Within her cell she meditated on the visions she had seen and wrote about them in *The Revelations of Divine Love*[8], now one of the great classics of spiritual literature.

Mother Julian has particular light to shed upon how we help other people with their problems through our intercessory prayer. First we must remember that God has been and is working in the situation which concerns us, long before *we* arrived on the scene. In the light of this we can with confidence take the particular issue which concerns us directly to God, letting our 'awareness' enter into it. In other words we become acutely alive to the situation itself within God's presence. When we have done this, we set the matter aside and continue to enjoy God's love. We believe that he is at work in the situation with which we have become involved.

Consider this saying of Mother Julian: "God is the still point at the centre: there is no doer but he".

Now enjoy *reading Isaiah 55:10 – 11*. He is at work in that situation which concerns *you* — and he will not fail.

FIVE   ANXIETY

There are some passages in the gospels I find hard to put into practice. The one I am suggesting to you now is just such a passage. *Read Matthew 6:25 – 34.*

I am by nature an anxious person. If my wife is late home I begin to wonder if she has had an accident. If the telephone rings very late at night, I automatically think it must be something serious.

How then do I make sense of this passage? It obviously cannot mean that we should not be concerned when something unfortunate happens to us or to someone we love dearly. This would be inhuman. What it may well mean is that we should try to avoid being *over-anxious* people who fear the worst in almost every situation.

May I share with you what has helped me to cope with my anxious nature?

A sense of humour. I often laugh at myself. Sometimes out loud! You see I have accepted that I am an anxious sort of person and I *have* to smile at the quite ridiculous contortions my mind creates.

A reminder that God loves me. I try to programme myself to come up with this basic affirmation when a particular anxiety has me in its grip. Yesterday we received help from Mother Julian. Here is another of her memorable sayings:

> *"Live gladly and gaily because of his love".*

SIX   PAIN

Pain is always a problem. No one likes to suffer pain and so we do all we can to avoid it. Modern medicine can control pain. The hospice movement which cares for those in terminal illness insists that life can be experienced right to the end — without severe pain.

That is good. But have we gone too far? Is pain — physical, emotional and spiritual — not a necessary element in our finding true fulfilment as persons?

Some illnesses from which we suffer, reflect the kind of people we are and the kind of lives we lead. If we just eliminate them with drugs or surgery and take no notice of the message they are trying to convey to us, we shall be depriving ourselves of greater self-understanding.

The same is true of emotional pain. Couples I have tried to help with marital problems have for years avoided the pain of recognising what was happening to their marriage. They have skated around their problem but never got to grips with it. Once they did — it hurt! But afterwards things could — and often did — improve!

Jesus knew that Calvary would be painful but "he set his face steadfastly to go towards Jerusalem".

Read John 12:25 – 26

SEVEN   LEARNING BY EXPERIENCE

Somebody 'above' thought it a good idea that I should be trained in how to broadcast on radio. I am still not sure why. The first thing I had to do was to give a brief talk and have it recorded and played back.

I was told that I was not good basic material. I have been 'preaching' for many years but, apparently, you don't preach on radio. You share with people those things which are real to you. You have to love the microphone and talk to it as though it were a person!

I was devastated. I thought I could give as good a radio talk as anyone and wondered why I'd never been asked!

However I took what my 'tutors' had to say with great seriousness and, on the second occasion, tried to put it into practice. I was told that I was 'getting better' and that there was hope!

Read 1 Corinthians 12:27–31. We each have gifts which God has given us to use. We must make the most of them. But one thing is sure. The way to be effective in the use of whatever gifts we each have is dependent upon our ability to absorb the next chapter *(1 Corinthians 13).*

To be trained in the 'school of love' is to be equipped to face many of life's problems and to discover the opportunities they provide.

5 AVAILABILITY

We are all "bound up in the bundle of life" and we all need each other. This statement is so obviously true that it need hardly have been made but how we actually become available to each other is an issue of vital importance. In this chapter we examine some of the negative ways in which people make themselves available — and then we shall go on to seek for a positive kind of availability, that which enables us, and the people to whom we become available, to grow and develop as human beings and as disciples of Jesus.

AVAILABILITY WITH STRINGS

We are all familiar with the classic situations where parents regard their children as properties. They want to live again through their children's success and so do all in their power to ensure that it happens — but it is their own conception of success which dominates the relationship. Such parents will give and give and give again — providing there is conformity!

The end result is usually disastrous. Some children comply with their parents' wishes but there is unexpressed resentment which may express itself in later years in depression or a lack-lustre life which continues to be dependent upon parents or parent figures, lacking any personal initiative and finding little joy or zest in living.

Others respond in an angry and bitter rebellion. The latter is often the more wholesome response. Because of it, dominating parents may begin to question their behaviour and realise their mistakes.

Some professional carers put fences round their availability which limit their effectiveness. Often this is associated with a manipulative form of control. The authority figure knows what is best for the client and 'moulds' him/her in that direction. There is no vibrant interplay of personalities and ideas. The flow is entirely in one direction — from helper to client. The end result may be some kind of behaviour improvement but it is likely to be of a flat and colourless kind. Older forms of spiritual direction were often based on this pattern as the very word 'direction' suggests. Those at the receiving end were given advice about methods of self-control and the subjugation of the flesh!

This kind of help is often given from behind a defensive wall. The helper needs the security of professional competence and the trappings of his profession — white coat, degrees, diplomas, clerical collar, etc. He/she is available but only on their own terms. Any attempt to discover the helper as a person is met with a polite refusal and studied rejection.

Teaching is sometimes offered in similar ways in educational institutions. It is seen as the imparting of knowledge rather than the provision of areas of meeting between teacher and pupils which can lead to the enlargement of experience. Students under pressure to obtain standards and qualifications sometimes opt for this kind of education. They want to know what will get them through rather than what will enable them to live!

AVAILABILITY FOR ITS OWN SAKE

I recall with immense gratitude a man who greatly helped me through my own teenage traumas. He was about twenty years older than myself but was near enough to the kind of experiences through which I was passing to be sensitive to them when he saw them being acted out in my life. He did not preach at me (although he was a professional preacher). He did not attempt to 'mould' me in a particular direction. Instead he provided me with an opportunity to share with him some of my fears, hopes and anticipations. He listened with evident interest and genuine understanding. Then he offered me the hospitality of his own experience. He told me about his own knowledge of the same kind of fears that I was enduring. He told me something of his own anxiety and the pressures which were upon him. (He was an outspoken pacifist and war was on the horizon.) He allowed me to question him; to challenge his motivations. In the end he influenced me more than any other person. He was, I believe, genuinely interested in me — not just as someone whom he could count as one of his successes but as someone about whose development as a person he was genuinely pleased.

One of the reasons why he gave me confidence was because he used to tell me that our conversations helped him. My telling of my boyish longings had caused him to re-live his own and see more clearly how his own life-direction had been formed. This was good news to me. It showed me that genuine availability is never a one-way traffic. It is the sharing of mutual experience from which both parties can benefit.

THE AVAILABILITY OF JESUS

Jesus was constantly available to people. Note the way he used his chance meeting with the woman he met at the Well of Sychar *(John 4)*. Jesus helped her to move forward to a deepening understanding of who she was herself and a growing realisation of who he was. When a relationship has been established (and the Bible record is surely a summary of a much longer conversation), he was ready to speak to her of his Messiahship.

Jesus also made himself available to his accusers. When the movement of events brought him within the shadow of Calvary he could have opted out — but he didn't. He was available to them to do with him as they pleased.

Even when he was on the cross itself, that same spirit was maintained. He was available to the malefactors and one at least responded gratefully. He was available to his mother and to his disciples and made arrangements for his mother's care and well-being.

In his earthly ministry he did have to get away from the crowds from time to time but this was in order to regather his strength so that he could return to the people to offer them friendship, enlightenment and healing.

CREATIVE AVAILABILITY

It has become quite commonplace in these days to stress the importance of *listening* but perhaps we have not yet explored fully the best kind of attitude on the part of the listener. Often a listener, be he/she a professional carer or just a friend, will develop a detached approach to the listening process. He is quiet and apparently receptive but he is only hearing at a superficial level. The atmosphere which is created by *disciplined listening* is a very real factor in any healing relationship. The person who needs help can find it by telling his/her story fully and freely to the one who is trying to be of assistance. But the listener is not just seeking for a perfect solution to pass on when the one who is unburdening himself or herself pauses or finishes the story. He is re-living his own experience in the light of what he is hearing. He himself is in a learning situation. Then when the opportunity arises, something of what the listener has discovered about himself is allowed to filter back into the conversation. Often this can give a sparkle and direction to the relationship which is helpful to both parties.

A mistake sometimes made is to be so full of our own enlightenment and vision that those who come to see us feel rejected because of their own inability to see things our way or to share in our kind of spiritual experience. All forms of religious enthusiasm are catching but some forms of fervent expressions of faith are repellent to certain kinds of people. Many who want for themselves the blessing which charismatics call "the fullness of the Spirit" are thrust into deep depression when it does not come to them in the same way others have received this gift.

To be aware of this danger is to realise the limitations of our own experience. Valid and important though it is for us, it is only part of the whole range of spiritual enlightenment that God can give. Out of our own acknowledgement of this to ourselves can come the basis for a deepening relationship with those who are seeking 'a closer walk with God'.

AN EXPERIENCE OF AVAILABILITY

I was once privileged to visit the Madonna House Community in Combermere, Northern Ontario, in Canada. I only knew one member of the community previously and her just slightly. Yet when I got there I felt a warmth of acceptance which had to be experienced to be believed. My wife, who was with me, shared the feeling that we were being enfolded in an embrace of love and care.

The secret seemed to emerge when we attended Mass. This was a carefully constructed service with the liturgy of the Holy Communion at the heart of the worship but surrounded by a freedom and spontaneity which arose out of the hearts and lives of the worshippers. I then realised why so many people go to Madonna House just to participate in this experience. They go with problems and anxieties and they are helped. The community members care for them and many are skilled in the practice of counselling — but in addition they provide the dimension of prayer in which every human situation and dilemma is given a Godward thrust by the dedication of the community members.

In the grounds there are little huts called *poustinias* (places of prayer). Members of the community go into these poustinias and stay alone for twenty-four hours with only bread and water for their diet and only the Bible for their enlightenment. Some members of the community live in the poustinias for several days each week but this is only for a few who feel called to do this on behalf of the others. One or two live permanently in a poustinia and give themselves to prayer and availability. We felt the impact of Madonna House upon our own lives.

One of the "words of the Lord" which came to the founder of the Community, Catherine de Hueck Doherty, and which are now included in *The Little Mandate* (the basis of the life of the Community) is this sentence: "Go without fear into the depths of men's hearts... I will be with you". That they are able to do this is because they have the ability to listen and to love.

It is not difficult to see how clearly availability is a stepping stone to maturity when you consider its opposite. Those people who live tight, circumscribed lives and who are available to no one in any real sense are caught up in a web of their own making. They fear to offer to another the hospitality of their own lives because they are afraid that such involvement will be too demanding and will restrict their own enjoyment of life. How wrong they are! Availability to others is of course costly in time and sometimes in emotional expenditure, but those who spend themselves in these ways get back just as much as — and indeed sometimes more than — they give. Honest, open relationships provide a two-way process which is a learning and enlightening experience for both parties concerned. To be available with the entire range of your own experience and to share the love which God has given to you is to discover greater depths within yourself and to come to know more, experimentally, about the true nature of God.

QUESTIONS FOR DISCUSSION

1. Discuss the following quotation from *The Significance of Jesus* by W. R. Maltby[9]: "Right to the end and never

more strikingly than in the difficult accounts of the resurrection experience this unique bestowing and refraining confronts us. These gifts that cease when they would have become bribes, these signs which persuade but never overwhelm, are the signature of Jesus on all his recorded deeds".

What does this quotation tell us about the availability of Jesus and what guidance does it give us about our own availability?

2. When you go to a professional 'carer' (doctor, social worker, counsellor, minister), what are you looking for? Share experiences and build up a picture of the ideal 'carer'.

3. A university professor said, towards the end of his long career, "I have discovered that my interruptions are my work". Do you feel any affinity with this statement?

Seven daily readings about Availability

ONE   **CREATING SPACE**

In *Tools for Meditation* by J. de Rooy[10] there is a superb meditation on the word "love".

Here is a small part of it:

> *To love is to create space*
> *where the other can be himself,*
> *it is enabling all his finest qualities to flower,*
> *helping him to find himself.*

Jesus did just this for his disciples. *Read John 14:5–14.*
Thomas and Philip were able to share their questionings
wiht him and to discover for themselves more about him.
There must have been many occasions unrecorded in the
gospels when Jesus made himself available and out of these
exchanges the disciples grew. Later their growing knowledge
was to be tested in the fires of adversity and they must have
then remembered some of those occasions when they had
shared their innermost thoughts and longings with him.

Remember with gratitude those who have 'created space'
for you. Do you set aside time to 'create space' for other
people? The wonderful thing is that when you do so, you
benefit yourself. Those who are in some kind of need often
give something to those who have made themselves available
to them. Wise doctors can learn from their patients!

Remember how Thomas responded in the end? "My Lord
and my God" (John 20:28).

TWO   ACCEPTANCE

Earlier in this chapter I refered to a visit my wife and I paid
to Madonna House in Combermere in Northern Ontario. As
we approached the house we passed a sign which said:
"There are no strangers here, only friends we are getting to
know better".

They were not idle words. We were strangers in the sense
that we had never been there before and had only a slight
acquaintance with one elderly person associated with the
community. But we felt totally accepted.

What does acceptance do to you? It creates trust. You feel
that you do not have to put on a mask and be what you are

expected to be. You can be who you really are. Within this sort of 'safe' relationship other things are possible. You can share fears and anxieties and you can explore your feelings. Had we been able to stay longer, this would undoubtedly have happened.

Jesus accepted people whom others despised. *Read Luke 7:36–50*. It is not easy to accept those who have defied the social norms. If our churches suddenly became flooded with 'sinners', what would we do? Would we really accept them?

Without being dramatic, try to demonstrate your acceptance of a person of whom you are slightly suspicious. The difference your new attitude makes may surprise you!

THREE   CARING

The basic meaning of this over-used word is to grieve, to experience sorrow and pain. We think of caring as being to relieve pain and provide some form of amelioration in distress. It is that but it is more. It is identifying with the person in need. It is feeling your way into his real self. There can be no real help without some form of identification.

I was a hospital chaplain for more than thirty-five years. I have often heard those who work in other disciplines speak of the importance of not getting involved. A proper professional detachment must be maintained.

Years ago I remember a very young hospital doctor who had been deputed to tell a close relative of a person's death. The patient had died suddenly and with no warning. The doctor was in tears. He felt it deeply. When he saw the patient's relative, he was still troubled. Yet in his own distress, and perhaps through it, he was able to help the bereaved person.

72

Another doctor friend told a patient that he was terminally ill. He was deeply moved and said to the patient: "I cannot help you very much but I promise that I will be with you". He was and it made all the difference.

I feel drawn to ask you to *read Isaiah 53:1 – 10* and invite you to reflect upon the title of a book about ministry by Henri Nouwen. It is called *The Wounded Healer*[11].

By his wounds we are healed... by our wounds, they?

FOUR   LOVE IN ACTION

Read Luke 8:40 – 56

After I had read this passage, I sat and thought about it. This came to me. Use it if it helps you but better still let the passage take hold of you and then write your own piece.

> *Many were waiting,*
> *one had a special need —*
> *his love, the light of his life*
> *lay dying.*
> *She was twelve years old.*

> *Jesus went with the man in distress,*
> *Jairus was his name.*
> *But before they reached the girl,*
> *another arm was outstretched towards him —*
> *at first no words — only the touch of trust.*
> *Jesus responded — but wanted to know*
> *who and why.*

73

Satisfied he moved on.
"The child is dead", they told him.
"Don't trouble any more."

But he did and
the child lived.

Loving brings people to life!

Try it!

FIVE   **STIMULATING QUESTIONS**

Availability is not only about helping people in their hour of
need and with their pressing anxieties. It is also about
getting people to ask questions about life — and that means
being people who ask questions ourselves.

A healthy Christian life has discovered some answers but it
also goes on uncovering new questions. Jesus was a fascinating teacher. He did not supply ready-made answers for his
hearers. Some things he was sure of — his Father's love, for
instance, and his own mission — but he knew that the best
way to win others was to get them asking the right
questions.

Read Matthew 5:1 – 12. Yes, this is one of the best known
passages in the New Testament. Don't turn to a
commentary to ask what these sayings mean. Let them speak
directly to you and make a note of all the questions they
raise in your mind.

I happen to know a little Welshman named Dai. (Yes, he
does exist!) He has spent his life getting other people to ask

questions: about politics, religion, philosophy, and social ethics. He is a pensioner now but the game goes on. He is a likable, lovable man who soon gets other people involved.

His secret? A zest for life and an insatiable curiousity.

If your being available means that people start asking the right questions, who knows? They may come up with some of the right answers. Right for them, that is. They may not necessarily be the same answers as yours.

SIX   YOUR FACE SAYS IT

When we meet people for the first time, we usually look at their faces. Afterwards when we are describing how we feel about them, it is often their faces and the expressions upon them which inspire our comments.

It was the German philosopher, Nietzche, who said of Christians: "I will believe in their Saviour when they look a bit more saved". Do you think that we followers of Jesus sometimes take ourselves a bit too seriously? We don't seem to really enjoy life and relationships. Our religion becomes a kind of inner censor which prevents us from having too good a time.

If our faith makes us attractive people it will show in our faces. And this has nothing to do with "putting on a face". That is a phrase we use to describe a 'cover-up', when we are hiding what we really feel by keeping ourselves under tight control.

Let your face say what you are feeling, be it joy or sorrow, happiness or pain. Be real. This is what matters.

A Bible scholar has written about "The human face of God". He referred of course to Jesus. *Read John 1:14–18.* Now let your imagination get to work. See his glory. Feel his presence. Receive his grace. When Moses came down from the mountain they said that "he was not aware that his face shone". Spend time with Jesus and it will show — in your face!

SEVEN   AVAILABLE TO ONESELF

Those who do business with others in the demanding work of pastoral care and counselling know how important it is to realise the significance of what is going on inside themselves. This is the reason why some form of supervision is necessary. It helps them to become more self-aware and saves them from falling into pitfalls.

One way of being available to oneself is through the creative use of silence. The way that I recommend is to practise the prayer of the heart. This is a method of silent prayer which uses a Bible word to quieten the mind. I have already referred to this practice in the introductory chapter on 'Awareness'.

In the silence things happen. The discomfort you felt in that relationship suddenly begins to be felt again. But now that you are detached from it, you understand better the anxiety which you felt about a certain aspect of your behaviour. Almost, as from nowhere, you get a clue to the truth about yourself. You begin to "make connections"!

Sometimes you will be discouraged and perhaps totally disillusioned. This is called "the dark night of the soul". When it happens, hang on. Those experienced in the spiritual life will tell you that it is almost always followed by a time of inner warmth and radiance.

Was Paul's 'dark night' expressed in Romans 7 and is his deliverance described in Romans 8? *Read Romans 7:14* right through to *Romans 8:11.* Try to visualise what happened to Paul. Could it happen to you?

6 STRESS

In these days and particularly within western, developed society a significant proportion of illness is attributed to an inadequate response to stress. In his book *The Diseases of Civilization*[12] the medical journalist, Brian Inglis, refers to the many illnesses which are no longer the 'killers' which they used to be — scarlet fever, diptheria, tuberculosis, pneumonia, meningitis, poliomyelitis. These have largely been conquered by a combination of improved public health measures and new and better drugs, particularly the antibiotics. He then goes on to point out that, in their place, there has been a considerable extension of what he describes as 'stress-related' diseases: heart attacks, strokes, hypertension, nervous illness and a general condition of unwellness which may give rise to accidents at work or on the roads; excessive indulgence in alcohol; recourse to drugs.

When he addressed the annual meeting of The Churches' Council on Health and Healing in 1986, Dr. Peter Nixon, an eminent cardiologist who has researched the links between coronary heart disease and stress, told us that a healthy response to stress includes the ability to adapt to new challenges and maintain sustained effort. However, if inner resources are inadequate, there is a point where fatigue develops and, if the outward pressure is still maintained, the tired mind and body cannot keep improving performance. This is likely to set in motion a downward curve which, if not acknowledged and faced, may result in one or other of the illnesses mentioned in the previous paragraph.

As part of his treatment for patients he believed had stress-related problems, Dr. Nixon offered the opportunity to spend a week or two living in a convent where they were helped to examine their life-style. He introduced them to methods of relaxation and meditation.

STRESS IS NECESSARY

It is however, important to realise that stress is necessary to our proper development as human beings. It is only as we are placed in a variety of stressful situations and respond adequately to them, that we make progress towards greater maturity.

It is evident that some forms of society are more stressful than others. Certainly our own society, in that it lays great emphasis upon personal achievement, can be exceedingly stressful for those who want to reach the higher echelons but who lack the resources and ability to enable them to do so. We do not all come into this world equally endowed physically, mentally and emotionally. The childhood years are formative as we saw in the chapter on 'Awareness'. Some are fortunate enough to be loved sensibly and grow up feeling secure in that love. Others are subjected to manipulative behaviour posing as love. This is meant as a statement of fact and is not to be seen as an excuse for being content with a low level of achievement. We each have to begin from where we are, that is the level we have reached from the starting point of our own original inheritance, but we must also acknowledge that this can be the means whereby we obtain the insights and resources which make greater progress possible.

The ways in which inadequate responses to stress damage our lives are many and various. One of the main ways is that the delicate balancing control known as the 'homeostatic mechanism' is disturbed. This can spark off all kinds of irregularities which can affect the digestive system, the bowel function, the cardio-vascular rhythm, the "nerves" etc. These symptoms may be treated by purely physical means, usually drugs, which may act as palliatives and even remove the symptoms. The danger is that unless the root problem is dealt with then those manifestations of illness may return either in the same or in another form. The real problem is, of course, ourselves; our personality make-up;

our lack of internal resources; our inability to secure helpful forms of support. We should not however, dismiss palliatives or refuse to take drugs. They may be necessary, both in the short and the long-term. The important thing is to deal more adequately with those deeper challenges which will enable our development as persons and as Christian disciples. The consequences of this can have profound effects upon our total well-being. Where do we begin?

BY ACCEPTING REALITY

One of the main difficulties in pastoral work is to help those who feel that, because they are Christians, they should not be the failures they believe themselves to be.

In one of those delightful devotional books, *Many Voices — One Voice*[13], Eddie Askew refers to a phrase he himself obtained from Monica Furlong, about "renouncing perfection for wholeness". This fits in with my own understanding of the meaningful Christian life which is not to be faultless but to be sincere in the ways in which we seek to serve God and our fellow human beings. When we examine ourselves honestly, we recognise that we do have faults and failings, but these we can accept because we know that God accepts us with them. This does not mean that we cease to strive to be better; it does mean that we stop accusing ourselves and feeling guilty. Our growing wholeness comes via the pathway of forgiveness for sin and failure. Wounds that have been healed leave scars behind — but these scars are an essential part of our growth towards maturity.

A monk was once asked about what happens within the monastery. His reply was: "We fall down and get up; we fall down and get up again!" This is certainly the reality of my own Christian life. When I am asked to define 'wholeness' my reply is always the same: "Wholeness is Jesus". My own growing wholeness depends upon my looking unto him (Hebrews 12:1–2).

It also helps me to recognise that there is a shadow side to my personality. It emerges in thoughts which arise unwanted from the unconscious mind; it comes out in some of my dreams; I recognise it in my jealousies and fears. My fear of death is associated with my unwillingness to let go of self. But recognising these signs of my shadow can be helpful. They can act as pointers to a healthier life-style and thought-life. They direct me to turn to Jesus at every conceivable opportunity. He knows that I have a shadow and that it is as necessary for my development as darkness is to light. I may hide some aspects of my life from closest friends, but I cannot — and I must not try — to hide anything from him.

This mention of my closest friends leads me to mention another challenge. We can get to know more about reality...

THROUGH BELONGING TO A SHARING GROUP

Our willingness to be vulnerable with specially chosen friends will depend upon the kind of people we are. Perhaps to belong to such a group is not for everybody but if we are so sure that it is not for us we should at least ask ourselves why we have arrived at such a conclusion! Members of a sharing group listen carefully to each other and are willing to share feelings as well as ideas and problems. Feelings govern our behaviour and attitudes far more than abstract, intellectual thought. We rationalise our actions often by making up our reasons for them after they have taken place. The real reason for what we have done lies in the realm of our feelings.

Those who are willing to share with others find that they get additional help with their daily living; have a sharper grasp of the problems and difficulties facing them; they also feel the strength of the support they receive from the other members of the group. I have belonged to several such groups and one of the most profitable was a group which contained a variety of theological views. I always feel more comfortable with people who think like I do — but they only serve to affirm my basic position and I need to be challenged. Sharing groups however, must have sufficient bonds to hold them together 'in Christ' and it is vital that every member respects the sincerity and integrity of the others. I have discovered more about my real self from those who disturb me than I have from those with whom I feel an almost total affinity.

There is yet another possibility open to us as we seek to respond adequately to stress. We can help ourselves further...

BY KEEPING A JOURNAL

A journal is a record in which we write down day by day or week by week the significant events in our lives, especially the times of challenge, the moments of discomfort and the sources of inspiration. A large desk diary is an admirable tool for such a practice. So many of our most creative experiences are lost because we do not take the trouble to keep a hold on them. We read a book and a sentence stabs us awake. We may underline it but even that may not be sufficient. The act of writing it down will help us to retain it in our minds, but even better than this — we now have a record. We can look back to it and our treasures are the more easily re-discovered.

But even more importantly situations arise which cause us worry and hurt. We agonise over them. We take certain actions but afterwards see that we made serious mistakes. Write down the details. Do not spare yourself. Remember however that you must also write down your successes. The events which turned out well because of the helpful way you had handled them. While all these things are happening, they naturally become part of your prayers. Thus insights will be sharpened; new discoveries will be made. A journal is a cheap form of psychotherapy but it is more than that. It is another chapter in the Acts of the Apostles — and this particular apostle in the midst is none other than *you!*

All these things will often come together in our Bible reading. If, as we have suggested in our Preface, the Bible is a conversation piece between man and God, the events in which we are involved are almost bound to be foreshadowed in scripture. Write down the connections. You will find in them the raw material of your daily living and your growth as a person. This is all part of your increasingly healthy response to stress.

This could then naturally move on to a further practice which will help us. This is...

THE CULTIVATION OF THE ART OF MEDITATION

Meditation has become suspect in some Christian circles because of its association in people's minds with various forms of Eastern religious systems. In particular the practice of Transcendental Meditation as taught by the Maharishi Mahesh Yogi has been attacked because it is said that the use of a Mantra to empty the mind of racing thoughts leaves a vacuum for dark and evil powers to enter. In fact the practice of Christian meditation goes right back to the earliest days of Christian history and particularly to the Desert Fathers in the second and third centuries. John Cassian (born c 360 AD) helped his followers to discover stillness within themselves by concentrating upon a scriptural phase. Julian of Norwich (c 1342 – 1420) was one of the most significant of the English mystics whose insights are being closely followed in these days. She saw the attributes of God as life, love and light and, her own writings having been re-discovered, they provide a rich source of meditative material.

The purpose of meditation is to still the mind and then to bring together the inspiration of scripture and the conflicts and concerns of the contemporary world. This sharpening of the mind with the wisdom of God helps us to see more clearly into the realities of complex situations and helps us to decide what we should do about them. Thus it is a vital element in our struggle to utilise the pressures of stress in creative ways. Through meditation we open up the channels along which the Holy Spirit can flow. All of us need to *"study to be quiet"* (1 Thess. 4:11).

ENDPIECE

The Christian life is a full life and we are often deeply involved in worldly things. Our times of withdrawal provide the resources with which we engage life's challenges. What God does promise is that he will be with us in the heart of the battle and will be available in a variety of ways "just when we need him most". By this means we shall grow and develop as persons through our stressful encounters. He has promised us victory and this he will surely give *(2 Cor. 2:14)*.

QUESTIONS FOR DISCUSSION

1. Let each member of the group spend a few minutes in silence recalling an extremely stressful situation and trying to re-experience the *feelings* aroused. Then share the feelings. Did you react positively? Where did you look for help? Other people? Prayer? Where did you find the support you desperately needed? Looking back, did you benefit from the experience?

2. Does the practice of medicine as you have experienced it

84

lay sufficient emphasis upon the stress factor? What do you know about the holistic approach? Is there any significance in the way the word 'holistic' is spelt ('holistic' as distinct from 'wholistic' occurs quite often in medical circles, i.e. The British Association for Holistic Medicine)?

3. Does your regular Sunday worship help you grow as a person? What kind of experiences would you wish your Church to provide so that you might be helped to "grow a soul"?

Seven daily readings about Stress

ONE   HELP FROM GEORGE HERBERT

You will need to read this poem by George Herbert through at least three times and then you will just begin to glimpse its meaning:

> *Prayer, the Church's Banquet, angel's age,*
> *God's breath in man returning to its birth,*
> *The soul in paraphrase, heart in pilgrimage,*
> *The Christian plummet sounding heaven and earth;*
>
> *Engine against the Almighty, sinner's tower,*
> *Reversed thunder, Christ-side-piercing spear,*
> *The six day's world transposing in an hour,*
> *A kind of tune which all things hear and fear;*
>
> *Softness, and peace, and joy, and love, and bliss,*
> *Exalted manna, gladness of the best,*
> *Heaven in ordinary, man well drest,*
> *The Milky Way, the bird of Paradise;*
>
> *Church bells beyond the stars heard, the soul's blood,*
> *The land of spices, something understood.*

The life to which we are called is union with God through Christ. *Read Colossians 4:2–6.* See the link between this passage and the poem. It is the 'heart in pilgrimage' which helps you to remain 'alert'. It is to spend time in 'the land of spices' which facilitates 'wisdom'.

How do the insights gained help you in your struggles with a stressful situation? When did you last discover "Heaven in ordinary"?

TWO   INNER HEALING

All of us carry a load of useless rubbish around inside ourselves! As we have seen, it is there from childhood days and through forgotten events which have happened since that time. When the rubbish is stirred by our being put under pressure strange feelings begin to rise: anger, resentment, annoyance. We often make the mistake of trying to trace these feelings back to more immediate events. There may be no direct connection but, in an obscure way, past happenings have triggered these unwelcome feelings.

Father William Hewett has written about Nicodemus in a song which is part of a recorded collection entitled *Where New Winds Blow*. Here are the two final verses:

> *Nicodemus through his tears*
> *Let go the anchor of the years,*
> *Sensed now the joy that comes with dawn,*
> *Breathed in the life of man reborn.*
>
> *So too with you if you would be*
> *Soul-sail filled, born anew, born free,*
> *Sail down the seas of all the years,*
> *Cast off in him all binding fears.*

Read the Nicodemus story again in John 3:1−21.

Let the 'stirrings' speak to you next time they happen. Try to recall how they may have begun. Then take them to Jesus. Use your imagination and feel his hand upon you. This is his word to you: "My son, my daughter, the past is forgiven; be at peace".

THREE   SUSTAINED BY THE SPIRIT

Baron Von Hügel was a master of the spiritual life and has helped many people through his writings. In one of his books he likens true prayer to sucking a lozenge!

I was taken aback when I read this because, when it comes to sweets, I confess to being a biter. No sooner is the sweet in my mouth than my teeth are breaking it in pieces and soon I have lost it. Better by far to take time to allow the sweet to circulate and flavour the saliva and so to last and last until at length you realise that it is no more.

The purpose of this chapter has been to stress the importance of quiet and meaningful reflection. As your mind is stimulated, so the Holy Spirit takes hold of the words and ideas and brings them to life within the context of your own background and experience.

Read Romans 8:26−27. When we are up against it and wondering if we can cope with the strains and stresses of life, the Holy Spirit comes to our aid. These verses suggest that, when we hit rock bottom, the Spirit then takes the initiative.

Now read verse 28. Yes, the raw wounds of life's darkest moments can be woven into our growing experience of wholeness. In this chapter we referred to Julian of Norwich. Perhaps the best known of her sayings is relevant here: "All shall be well and all manner of things shall be well". Hallelujah!

FOUR   THE TREADMILL

Do you remember taking exams and then waiting anxiously for the results? If we did well, then we are pleased with ourselves and it is pleasant to be congratulated by our friends and relations.

This is good. To succeed and be well thought of by others is a satisfying experience. All of us like it. After all, as we often say, we are only human.

But it can lead to a disastrous way of life and to a burden of stress thay may ultimately break us. If we are not careful, we can come to live only by what we achieve and this means that, when one goal is reached, another must be established. And then another... and another... If, as must eventually inevitably happen, we do not quite live up to our anticipations, it can mean that we begin to lose our self-esteem. So we drive ourselves, notching up our successes and trying even harder when we seem likely to fail.

There is a better way. We can find peace with God and within ourselves when we know that we are accepted by God and loved by him and our fellow human beings simply for *what we are.*

1 John 4:7−21 is our charter. Here is set out the basis of the Christian life:

> *He loves us — we are accepted.*
> *We love our brothers and sisters — they are accepted.*

This knowledge takes us off the treadmill and puts us safely on to the escalator!

FIVE   THE CHALLENGE OF CHOICE

Each day brings its own series of choices: to initiate this particular action: to face up to this problem; to tackle a difficult relationship.

But there is always a choice. We can defer action. We can refuse to face a problem in the hope that it will go away (it will not). We can continue to endure a difficult relationship by keeping it at a superficial level.

These are the kind of choices we have to make day by day. But there are many others. What kind of attention do we give to people we regard as nuisances? (A 'nuisance' may in fact be a very needy person.) What kind of discipline do we ourselves impose upon our use of time? Choices... Choices... Choices...

We would do well to remember that we are what we choose. We grow in stature by the quality of our moral choices. Every difficult decision we make and which, in our hearts, we know is right, enhances and strengthens us as persons. We become less adequate when we refuse to face reality.

Read Ephesians 4:25—32. The "new life in Christ" is a life in which there are many choices to be made. For every positive virtue outlined here, there is also a negative possibility. You are called to live as Christ lived and lives. *Does the secret lie in Chapter 5: 1—2?* When your will is "controlled by love", you are on your way.

There are some hard sayings in the New Testament. *Take Romans 12:14 – 21 for instance.* Pretty tough going this and yet how relevant! It happens to us all sooner or later. We meet someone in business, leisure activity, the local Church — and they *are* difficult to get on with! They rub us up the wrong way and 'grate' on us. What we often try to do is to avoid them, but sometimes we cannot. By the very nature of our social situation we have to meet them from time to time.

Has it ever occurred to you that difficulties in relationships may have as much to say about our weaknesses as theirs? It often happens that two extroverts find it hard to get on together. Both have a need to be 'top-dog'. So the first question to ask is: "Why what is going on between us makes me feel insecure?".

This may mean discovering something about yourself which you find disturbing. Be thankful for that. To realise it may be the means of your doing something about it. In this way our awkward relationships can provide us with valuable experience for living. We should not then try to avoid them but utilise them for our own development and for the ultimate good of the other person concerned. As Fred Kaan writes:

> *Let Christian people practice praise and love*
> *and let the clearness of their actions prove*
> *that Jesus Christ is well and living.*

Does what Paul says in our passage for today really work? There is only one way to find out!

Here are some wise words written by St. Francis de Sales in his *Treatise on the Love of God*[14]:

> *Every meditation is a thought but every thought*
> *is not a meditation.*

> *When we think about the things of God not to learn*
> *but to kindle our love, that is called meditating.*

Although the Bible is not the only source of ideas and images for meditation, it is undoubtedly the richest mine of treasure of this kind. This is because it is a book about God's search for man and man's search for God.

When you meditate on scripture, as you are being invited to do every day in this series of readings, ask yourself about the meaning of the words in their original, historical setting. What do they tell you about the purpose of God's love for those in whose day the words first came alive?

Then ask yourself what these words have to say to you and to your situations. Read yourself in between the lines. With regular practice you will be able to detach yourself from the clamant pressures of the world and "behold the glory of the Lord". This is not however just to enjoy an esoteric 'trip'. It is to become more sensitively aware both of your own and other people's needs.

Now work this out with Philippians 4:4 – 9. Verse 6 suggests what may seem to you to be quite impossible (it does to me!). But take the passage as a whole and try to put as much as you can into practice. Then verse 6 may seem less like an unclimbable mountain!

91

7 CREATION

We tend to think of creation as having to do with the beginnings of life as we know it, human, animal, vegetable, mineral. Once God had set the world in motion then this was the end of creation. Hence we refer to the stories about beginnings in the early chapters of Genesis as the 'Creation' stories. It was the Deists who believed that God set the world going like a man winding up a clock and then left it to its own devices.

This is however a limited view of creation for those who live in post-resurrection days. We have been assured that "if anyone is in Christ, he is a new creation" (2 Cor: 5:17). God sending Jesus to us and the manner of his life and death and rising again is our guarantee that creation is a continuous process. This is cause for rejoicing.

One of the earliest Christian heresies was Gnosticism. The Gnostics believed that the body was evil and that it was the tomb of the soul. *We* know that this is not true and we gladly affirm creation — including our physical beings. We can delight in our sexuality, for instance, and see it as an essential feature in God's continuing, creative activity. We delight in form and beauty and we utilise the gifts of art and music and literature in our worship. The sensual and the spiritual are not opposed to one another; they are both essential elements in God's creative plan. His purpose for our lives is a delicate blending of the sensual and the spiritual components. Where there is balance and the cross-fertilisation of the one by the other, there is growth and development. Where one is over-emphasised at the expense of the other, there is a stifling of an essential element without which our own re-creation will be stunted and warped. Some would place fearful restrictions around our sensual appreciation through an obsessive concern for things spiritual. When, in the stories of Genesis, God saw *all* the world that he had made, he declared it to be "very good" (Genesis 1:31).

CREATION AND SALVATION

Creation and Salvation are closely related. Michael Wilson in *A Coat of Many Colours*[15] suggests that "a new balance between ideas related to creation and salvation needs to be established... Salvation is connected with the immediate correction of a particular deviance, creation is a long term process". This suggests that salvation is part of the creation process. It is about putting things together and thus restoring them to their original function. This is a vital factor in the healing process. What doctors call *homeostasis* is the delicate balancing mechanism which enables human beings to function healthily. When it is disturbed by self-abuse, wrong thinking or just plain sin, the outcome is often an illness of one kind or another. Salvation experience restores the creative process and can bring renewed health and vigour. It restores the balance; it is a deep and profound inward experience which has powerful overall consequences.

TRANSFORMATION

This happened to Margaret (not her real name). She was disabled with a badly twisted body but an attractive, open face. She had lived in a variety of homes but she was hungry for love. She particularly wanted to be married and her over-eagerness spoiled one relationship after another. In despair she half-attempted suicide and, as a result, found herself in group therapy. Some of the group were physically disabled; others were there because of their anxiety or depression.

First she had to learn about making relationships 'without strings'. She discovered how to appreciate other people without wanting to use them to satisfy herself. She came to see people as having value in their own right and it became possible for her to give and receive love because this was a good thing in itself. Life began to take on an entirely new meaning. Creative gifts were released and she soon began to help others. She was 'born again', although not in any narrow sense. She was a person being made whole. Someone introducing her to another person described her as having 'got it together'. Then almost by accident she met a suitable potential life-partner and fell in love. This time the relationship was allowed to take its own course. There was no rush and no pressure. It worked out and today she is not only a contented wife but also a caring mother. She was and is a practising Christian and her faith has come alive too. Previously her faith had been a crutch; now it has become a launching pad and is an essential part of her contribution to God's creation.

CREATIVE SPIRITUALITY

Meister Eckhart was a Dominican mystic and prophet born in Germany in 1260. He developed a fine, holistic spirituality which combined the mystical element with a robust concern for social justice. In an article in *A Dictionary of Christian Spirituality*[16], Father Matthew Fox OP explains Meister Eckhart's four-fold path.

It began with the positive approach *(Via Positiva)*. This is about joy and rapture. Eckhart saw God as making all things new. He visualised God as "a great underground river that no one can dam up and no one can stop". The word of God is creative energy. It stirs, stimulates and enlarges the mind and the spirit. Such activity calls for constant gratitude and praise.

This positive outlook is then complemented by "Letting go and letting be" *(Via Negativa)*. This healthy self-abandonment into Divine reality is the way we have direct experience of God's love and grace. We rely upon it; we 'let go' into God. This does not mean the mortification of our natural instincts; it does mean that the passions of anger and desire are directed in the ways we need to travel. His teaching was light years ahead of his time but is now supported by more modern psychological concepts.

The third way is that of 'birthing' *(Via Creativa)*. This is entirely positive. It is neither spiritual 'navel-gazing' nor virile action without any adequate foundations. 'Birthing' is akin to an infusion of grace. The initiative is with God as we saw in the chapter on 'Invasion', but then creative 'birthing' is an ongoing process. God's power stimulates our own innate (God-given) powers and so we give birth to a new life in individuals and in the community.

The final way is about building a new and more just society by way of exercising creative compassion *(Via Transformativa)*. This compassion is not just felt but acted out in society. It is a reiteration of the Biblical truth that faith without works is dead (see the Epistle of James). This vital truth has to be celebrated as well. "Praise", said C. S. Lewis, "is inner health made audible". For Eckhart this audibility was demonstrated through practical deeds of compassion which included challenging established authority.

Taken as a compendium of teaching, Eckhart's system illuminates and illustrates the comprehensive nature of a real spirituality which is creative in all its effects. In his lifetime he received ecclesiastical censure but in 1980 the Dominican Order requested Rome to lift all the censures laid upon him. It was a long overdue recognition of a down-to-earth saint.

CREATIVE RELATIONSHIPS

Our lives are lived in and through our relationships. There is a time for solitariness but there is no such thing as solitary Christianity. Yet we do not give a lot of thought to relationships until there is a serious breakdown affecting our personal happiness. We often take relationships for granted, enjoying those which are naturally pleasurable and avoiding those (if possible) which we feel threaten us or we do not like. In fact it is the very relationships that we find difficult which, in the end, can prove to be most useful, both to our own development and to the enrichment of community life.

Think first about why you enjoy the relationships which have come to mean much to you. Is not an element in them the fact that the other person appreciates *you* and has made that clear in one way or another? Might some of the difficult relationships you now endure be changed by a deliberate change of attitude on your part? Anthony Storr in *The Integrity of Personality*[17] points out that maturity in personal relationships demands that we do not overwhelm other people or treat them as less than persons. Nor should we allow ourselves to be 'taken over' or absorbed by the other person, however powerful a personality he or she may be. Instead "each shall contribute towards the affirmation and realisation of the other person".

Let us assume that the initiative in improving relationships is in our hands. A good place to begin is to recognise our own tendency to be critical without any thought about the problems and difficult life situations which surround 'the other person'. This in itself can bring about a change of attitude. From this point we move on to look out for the opportunities to care for them in positive and constructive ways.

HELP FROM ST. PAUL

Galatians 6:1–5 gets to the heart of the matter. Its key thoughts are gentleness in understanding; a sensible view of self; an awareness of the other's needs and a quiet determination to do something about them. Note the juxtaposition of the two sentences, "Help carry one another's burdens" (v2), and "Everyone has to carry his own load" (v5). They seem to be saying the opposite but not so.

We must not attempt to take responsibility away from the other person. We cannot make up their minds for them. Indeed we can help them to have the confidence to carry their own burdens by encouraging them to see that they can contribute towards the enrichment of our lives. We then help them to carry their own by being by their side and, as we have seen in another chapter *available* to them.

In Dag Hammarskjold's *Markings*[18], there is a moving account of a particular person's failure within an organisation for which he had responsibility. He had failed and had broken down but, when the final scene occurred, the unfortunate man said through his tears: "But why did you never help me? Why did you never tell me what to do? ...One day I remember I was so happy; one of you said something that I had produced was quite good". Dag Hammarskjold's comment on this sad situation was: "It is always the stronger who is to blame. We lack life's patience". Words of honest appreciation coupled with thoughtful guidance and even gentle criticism might have brought about a change in that man's attitude and led him to success. The actual outcome was that he was destroyed.

As I write, a dear friend has recently died. People travelled from far and wide to be at his Thanksgiving Service. I was not surprised. The same kind of openess and tender care which Arthur had shown in his relationship with me he had shared with many others. Even those who only met him briefly recognised his genuine sincerity. He always looked for the best in others and was never slow to express his appreciation. Those to whom he was still giving pastoral care were devastated by his passing. He was a truly genuine and authentic person and his influence is continued in the many people he had helped through his creative relationships with them. He was a partner in God's continuing creation.

ENDS AND BEGINNINGS

Life is made up of a series of 'ends' before the final ending we call "death" arrives on the scene. These 'ends' come in widely differing packages: children leaving home; redundancy at work; bereavement; retirement; sudden and unexpected change. Yet because of God's continuing creation each experience, even the most tragic ones, contain within them the seeds of hope.

A friend trying to encourage me in my own retirement told me that his retirement had proved to be the most creative period of his life. Previously he had been on a kind of treadmill. He had worked in order to live and provide for his family. Now he had been able to cultivate a long dormant artistic gift and give more time to other people. He had set about this with deliberate intent and it had worked out splendidly. "I feel now", he told me, "that I shall die a much happier person because of what has been possible in what I call my twilight years." And beyond death the Christian hope points us on to yet another 'new creation'.

A final point is that God's continuing creation is active within suffering. Harry Williams underlines this in *The True Wilderness*[19] when he insists that "We can know the power of Christ's resurrection only if we know the fellowship of his sufferings". Dietrich Bonhoeffer could write from the prison, where he knew suffering and was to face death, and encourage a young friend in these words: "Take care of yourself and make the most of the beautiful country you are in. Spread *hilaritas* around you and mind you keep it yourself!"

God's continuing creation is a challenge to us to be part of it through our own creativity. This will only be possible if we keep in close touch with our Creator.

QUESTIONS FOR DISCUSSION

1. Let each member of the group (if willing) share a significant experience they felt was creative in their lives. Then discuss the factors which made that experience creative. Where did God come in? How did that experience facilitate your own growth and development? How did it affect others?

2. Does Meister Eckhart's fourfold path mean anything to you? Think about phrases like "tapping into God's creation"; "letting go into God's love"; and the quotation from C. S. Lewis, "Praise is inner health made audible".

3. Think about a person you like and with whom you have a good relationship. Then think about a person you don't like and with whom you have a bad relationship. What made the difference? Was it all their fault? Is it possible to set about improving difficult relationships and, if so, how?

Seven daily readings about Creation

ONE   IN SEARCH OF MEANING

A University Director of Student counselling expressed concern because so many clients seemed to be unable to cope with life since it had lost all meaning. "I feel adrift upon an endless ocean of relativity", said one of them.

Is it too simplistic to suggest that Jesus is the one who gives a whole series of clues to life's meaning and purpose? Some would say so but I just want to make that assertion. However I do not make it blindly; I make it because I honestly believe it to be true. His attitude towards other people seemed just right. He was not afraid to condemn falsity and spurious living, but, at the same time, he was always ready to bind up any wounds he had inflicted. His one aim was that through coming into contact with him, others should find wholeness.

Then there was his own trust in his Father's love. It had to face severe testing. There could be no greater trial than that endured on Calvary. But he won through and now offers us a share in his victory.

Like Victor Frankl in *Man's Search for Meaning*[20] I believe that "the salvation of man is through love and in love". And this insight comes direct from Jesus — the man for others.

Read Galatians 1:11 – 24. Here are the notes I have written beside this passage in my wide-margined Bible: "Tremendous drive; inner restlessness; God took the initiative; Paul responded; went away for reflection; came back, took counsel and began his life's work". How do these experiences relate to your own pattern of response?

TWO   CHALLENGE FROM TAIZE

In the seventies forty thousand young people met at Taizé in Southern France. They sent a message to the whole Church of Christ and it contained these compelling sentences: "Are you at last going to become a 'universal community of sharing' ...a place of community and friendship for the whole of humanity? Are you going to become the 'people of the Beatitudes', having no security other than Christ, a people poor, contemplative, creating peace, bearing joy and a liberating festival for mankind?"

The implications are plain. The gospel not only has to be preached. It has to be lived. In order to convince men and women of the essential 'rightness' of following Jesus, we must live out our faith and *show* to people what it means.

Might this begin for us when we truly celebrate and give thanks for every creative development and growing insight which comes to us? Have we lost the art of truly joyous celebration? Genuine thanksgiving seems somehow to inscribe our discoveries upon our hearts in indelible ink.

Have you discovered anything recently about the paramount importance of 'quality of life'? Did you cultivate a 'thanksgiving response' when it happened? What a vital difference it makes to worship when we all come with something specific for which we want to thank God.

Read Colossians 3:12−17. Here you have inward experiences (awareness of God's love); outward expressions (compassion, kindness, being helpful and forgiving...). Then comes the phrase which holds the whole passage together, "And be thankful". The final verse (17) of this passage is tremendously searching. An adequate response certainly furthers God's continuing creation!

THREE   WHO AM I?

Who am I? is the title of a poem by Dietrich Bonhoeffer. It reveals basic inner conflict which all of us experience in one way or another — the difference between the person I show to the world and the person I know I really am within.

Bonhoeffer had a reputation for courage, for calmness, for the ability to face each worsening situation with strength of mind and purpose. He bore "the days of misfortune, equably, smilingly, proudly, like one accustomed to win".

But there was another Bonhoeffer. He was sometimes "weary and empty at praying, at thinking, at making, faint and ready to say farewell to it all".

Writing the poem was, in all probability, a tremendous relief. Sometimes we try to keep a 'stiff, upper lip' too long. To acknowledge one's weakness can be a sign of strength. Bonhoeffer was a strong man, well disciplined in mind and body. And the poem ends upon a note of trust: "Whoever I am, thou knowest, O God, I am thine".

Paul experienced the same kind of dual personality (don't we all?). *Read Romans 7:14 – 8:1.* During a time of inward conflict I read this passage and wrote in my prayer diary: "Accept the struggle; affirm the positive; be prepared for set-backs". Bonhoeffer's deep spirituality saw him through at the end. Almost his last words were contained in a message sent to his trusted friend, Bishop Bell: "Tell him that for me this is the end, but also the beginning". It was this quality of life revealed in Bonhoeffer's struggles and victories which has given added depth to his influential theological reflection.

FOUR   **STATIONARY PILGRIMAGE**

Read Hebrews 12:1 – 2.

A pilgrim, according to the Dictionary, is one who "is going somewhere in fulfilment of a vow". This implies movement towards a goal. A pilgrim has a destination in mind and is steadily moving in that direction. These verses suggest that the goal is Jesus himself; it is this 'mystical union' which links us with God's continuing creation.

But this aspect of the Christian pilgrimage must of necessity include times of 'standing still'. How are these two parts of the journey related? Surely the one equips us for the other. It is only as we take time to 'stand still' that we make progress.

In her poem *The Keys of the Kingdom*[21], Monica Furlong describes a journey that moves inward from the city to the street, to the lane, to the yard, to the house, to the room, to the bed..." And on that bed a basket of sweet flowers". At the heart of all things there is beauty, serenity, peace.

But that inward journey must now be taken in reverse, from the bed back to the city. The treasures contained within "the basket of flowers", which represent the "still point of the turning world", must now be shared with others who live among many strains and tensions "in the city".

This is why we must make our 'stationary pilgrimages'. We must 'stand still' in order to be meaningfully active. We must "study to be quiet".

I like Alan Dale's translation of *1 Corinthians 13:4: "Love is never in a hurry"*. It is not always the terribly busy people who are being most creative. The musical pauses are an essential part of the symphony.

FIVE   RIGHT DISCERNMENT

Here is a verse from a song by Father William Hewett taken from *Cave of Living Streams*[22]:

Know in your life what lasts and grows,
Choose the better way he shows,
Don't grab everything, whoever can?
Discern what will last — and choose God's love in man.

As we look back on the years we have had, the truth of that verse will come to life in past experience. The things that last are the things which help you to grow.

Trust

This is not always easy. Things go wrong. Expectations fade. Disappointments take over. To keep on trusting requires effort. It does, but it is always worthwhile. To give way to bitterness is to spoil ourselves and to harm those nearest to us.

Hope

To keep hope alive sometimes requires all the courage and moral fibre we can muster. We often have to look hard to see what there is to hope in and to hope for. But there is always something, or rather, someone!

Love

This is the better way. To choose love is to have all that we really need. This is what lasts and endures for ever and ever.

You have already heard it suggested but try it out again: *Read 1 Corinthians 13* and replace the word love with 'I'. Getting to the heart of this passage helps us to discern the wheat from the chaff; the good from the bad; the true from the false. It is all summed up in another quote from Father William Hewett: "The need is not for more knowing about prayer but for a prayerful kind of knowing".

To be part of God's ongoing creativity is to find fulfilment in life. Dr. Martin Israel in *Summons to Life*[23] lists four factors in the discovery of fulfilment:

A Humble Heart

In life we often feel slighted. Something happens to us which we resent. A proud heart hits back and tries to wound and hurt. A humble heart seeks to accept and learn something from the experience.

An Adventurous Spirit

The development of the spiritual life offers rich opportunities for adventure. Do not be satisfied with yesterday's devotional practices. Try something new as well as utilising all that is best in the old.

A Questioning Mind

Children learn a great deal by persistent questioning. We should carry on asking questions all our lives. This does not mean constantly raking over our 'quiet certainties', but it does mean allowing the mind and intellect free rein.

A Vibrant Body

Our bodies need proper use and proper care. This means regular exercise and a good diet. To begin your prayer time with simple relaxation exercises is to link body, mind and spirit in creative harmony.

Now trace a similar pattern in Hebrews 12:1–7. We are all running in the Marathon. It is tough going but there is refreshment and encouragement to be found at various stages on the way. Each brings its own pattern of fulfilment — and way out there is the finishing tape which marks not the end but a new beginning.

Think just for a moment of a person whom you feel is damaging his or her own life. Is the problem total self-centredness? Or irrational anxiety? Or pre-occupation with success and recognition?

If you reflect upon it you may feel that it is because of tunnel vision. They are concentrating upon one aspect of life to the exclusion of all others. Their life force is being thrust into one narrow area of living. The consequence is that they are only partly alive.

Fully alive people spread themselves around. Their interests are wide and expansive. They cultivate interests appropriate to each stage of life. They are probing deeply into the questions of faith and life and they value other people's experiences.

At the same time they have their sheet anchors. They have come to believe in certain fundamental truths which they live by and put into practice. They are not unwilling to revise their views when new insights come.

Above all they exercise their emotions. They are not afraid to be vulnerable. They feel deeply and share their love with those they instinctively like and with those who need it most.

Read 2 Corinthians 4:7–15. Look for "spiritual treasure" (7). Recall the cross for through his death we live (10). Life is 'at work' within doing what yeast in the dough does for bread.

Now read John 17:3 and John 20:31. The word translated 'life' is *vita.* Play a devotional game of word associations.

8 DISCIPLINE

When I was a student I participated in a rebellion! It was in the immediate post-war years and most of us had been in one form of National Service or another. In the pre-war years theological students had tended to be younger and lacking in wider experience of the world. They were treated rather like grown-up schoolboys (yes, males only in those unenlightened days!). The rule had been that all authority was vested in the staff and, if you did not like it that way, then you should not be there. *We* didn't like it but we felt that we should be there. We wanted to be treated as responsible adults who were allowed some say in the way college life was organised. We tried reasonable representation but when this failed, we rebelled!

Today others enjoy the fruits of our protest because the situation is different. Some would say there is not enough difference, but there is an easier relationship between staff and students. There is opportunity for students to be involved in the way the college is run, and the rules to be observed are generally simple and acceptable. Discipline is not imposed from above in an arbitrary manner; the guide lines have been mutually agreed because this is in the best interests of all concerned. Hopefully it is the discipline of discipleship.

The fact that the words *discipline* and *discipleship* share the same root is interesting. A disciple is one who responds to an invitation (Mark 1:17), and is then helped to realise all that is involved in the life of discipleship (Mark 8:34 – 35). If it is to work, this discipline has to be freely accepted and then applied to every aspect of the Christian life.

THE DISCIPLINE OF SELF-CONTROL

Politicians when bemoaning juvenile delinquency and the rising crime rate among young people tend to blame inadequate parental control. While this is sometimes an excuse to cover up inadequate provision in education and social services (plus youth unemployment), there is sufficient truth in the allegation to merit careful investigation. Undisciplined children frequently come from homes where there has been correction and punishment of all kinds — slapping, denial of privileges and rewards and so on. The problem is that the very discipline itself has been applied in an undisciplined way. Threats are made but are not kept. Then, for no good reason the parent comes down with an unnecessarily heavy hand. Parents who operate on the "do as I say and not as I do" basis are storing up trouble for the future as well as creating unwelcome friction in the present. Consistency is essential in the setting and application of simple rules and boundaries. There must also be mutual agreement about the ways in which they are applied between mother and father because a child soon recognises how easy it is to play off one against the other if there is a lack of co-operation in the parental camp.

The only basis for future self-discipline is that of example and unselfish love. Example, because when children see parents working away at their own relationships and facing up to their differences with courage and tenacity, this makes an abiding if unconscious impression. Love is demonstrated when parents spend time with their children and go to the trouble of explaining the actions which have been queried. This encourages young people to grow up with a proper appreciation of themselves and provides the foundations for them to tackle adequately the challenges they will face in later years.

Two boys grew up in a home where Dad died early after a lingering illness. Today they have precious memories of shared suffering and the confidence and trust in each other displayed by their parents. The outcome has been their heightened sense of responsibility for their mother's welfare and their displaying a maturity beyond expectation in their application to study and choice of careers.

But if so much depends upon childhood experiences, what about those who did not get such a good start in life? Those who came from homes which lacked this stability and where 'love' was expressed in selfish, manipulative ways?

GOD'S FATHERHOOD

Some of those who consciously feel themselves to be in that positon will give up easily and in mitigation "pass the buck" to their parents. This is the negative aspect of psychological insights and provides the basis for jokes about criminals who attempt to excuse their deviant behaviour by pointing to their unfortunate childhood experiences. The answer surely is that, although we all begin from different positions in the starting block, we must all endeavour honestly to recognise precisely where we are and work at life from that particular vantage point. For those of us whose lives are set within the context of Christian discipleship, there is the possibility that grace can help to make up for what we have lacked. A direct awareness of God's Fatherhood can help to create confidence and inward security. The Bible reveals, in so many different passages, how that God loves needy people (see Hosea 11 and Luke 15). As we respond to that love, the discipline we freely accept begins in gratitude. To become aware that we are loved is to come alive. To continue purposeful living and to hold on to what we have received involves us in the discipline of discipleship. This means facing the real issues of life and doing something constructive about them.

I recall stages in my own life when I had problems. I recall being distressed and annoyed because my life-plan was not working out as I thought it should. I was resentful. It was always 'the other person' who was to blame. The change came when I joined a delightful group of people who met regularly to share thoughts *and feelings* with one another. This group helped me to see that difficult situations do not go away. I had to work at them. It was tough going and I shed many tears and had many sleepless nights. In the end certain things began to work out and I look back to my membership of that group as a seminal time in my life. The group helped me to realise that I was loved and that there were resources available to me in my troubles. Simple changes helped me — like doing the things I did not like doing before turning to the things I enjoyed. This helped me to be more disciplined in the way I used my days and planned my time. Also I tried to bring God into the planning and into the way I worked. Previously God had been a kind of decorative backcloth. Now he was involved — and I was all the better for it.

THE DISCIPLINE OF ATTENTION

Dr. Jack Dominian, the well known Christian psychiatrist, was giving a lecture at a Conference arranged by the Institute of Religion and Medicine in September, 1989. He pointed out that we Christians have a great deal to say about love but are not always good at showing it in our daily living. He challenged us to demonstrate how we put love into action by 'facilitating relationships'. He spoke of this in relation to marriage and indicated the comparatively short time it takes to "fall in love" but which is followed by decades of interaction in marriage. This is what we have to work at and it requires — as in other areas of life — the discipline of attention.

This is also called for when we face up to apparent failure. When this happens we must pay special attention to the reasons for our failure. Realisation and acknowledgement can often be the gateway to new initiatives which make for growth and progress. Prior to May 24th, 1738 John Wesley felt that he was a failure. After the Aldersgate experience he knew that God truly loved him and this gave rise to one of the most disciplined and fruitful lives in the history of Christendom.

THE DISCIPLINE OF FORGIVENESS

Paying attention to situations which call for forgiveness is also a challenge to discipline. Dr. Una Kroll was also a speaker at the same Institute of Religion and Medicine Conference I have just mentioned. She referred to an article by one Raymond Studzinki entitled *Remember and Forgive* which she had discovered in an issue of *Concilium* (April 1986). He suggested in his contribution that the following conditions are necessary for forgiveness to operate:

(a) The recognition of situations requiring forgiveness
(b) An intention and decision to forgive
(c) An ability to 're-member' the incident in order to digest it and make it a part of one's history
(d) An acceptance of one's own need for forgiveness
(e) A willingness to start a new relationship with the person who is forgiven.

What a difference would be made to a variety of situations — personal and social; national and international — if there was closer attention paid to the possibilities of initiating forgiveness.

THE DISCIPLINE OF A SIMPLE RULE

Most religious communities live by a Rule. This is usually formulated at the time the community comes into being and is then adjusted and amended as the years go by and developments proceed. Such Rules have to do with the way in which authority is exercised and decisions made; the basis on which new members are accepted and the procedures to be gone through at that time. There is also a Rule if a member wishes to leave the community. Then there will be the commitment of the different members to each other; the ways in which leaders are appointed or elected, and what must happen to resolve differences and conflicts. Finally there will be set out the pattern of prayer, worship and meditation to be followed by community members. This will include the times of worship including the celebration of the Eucharist, and the periods of private prayer, study and meditation.

Many individual Christians find help in committing themselves in fellowship to others, often on a temporary basis as in a modern Ashram. This will include a form of sharing possessions and commitment to prayer and service. The Franciscans have a Third Order for those who live in their own homes and exercise their discipleship through their own jobs and within their local churches. It is however a searching Rule and there is a procedure to be followed by those who wish to join. There is no automatic acceptance.

Many of us try to live by a self-imposed Rule which is within our capabilities and which we feel will help us in our Christian commitment without being too legalistic. It will include a commitment to a time of prayer each morning and possibly evening as well. Tithing one's material resources may be a feature of our Rule. Then there may be a pledge to consult regularly with a Spiritual Director or Soul Friend. More and more people are discovering the value of this even if it is only on three or four occasions each year.

THE RULE OF ST. BENEDICT

The way in which an ancient Rule can be beneficially explored by those of us living in a wider community is provided for us by Esther de Waal in her exposition of the Way of St. Benedict. Her delightful book is called *Seeking God*[24]. She sums up the various aspects of the Rule in a series of words which in themselves provide food for thought and meditation. They are:

> *Listening*
> *Stability*
> *Change*
> *Balance*
> *Material Things*
> *People*
> *Authority*
> *Praying*

A consideration of each one can have fascinating consequences but I am particularly drawn to the word *balance*. For St. Benedict this was "the rhythmic succession of those three elements prayer, study, work". The intention of St. Benedict in drawing up his Rule was that it should call for "nothing harsh, nothing burdensome".

It is his principle of moderation in all things which appeals to me. The development of faith and holiness is the aim of the Rule of St. Benedict and this applies to those of us who live our lives as ordinary citizens in the community. Our aim is not a sequestered holiness (nor was theirs). We enjoy the things that are good (Philippians 4:8 – 9) — music, poetry, art, drama, gardening, eating, friendly company. These and many other things are part of the good life. When details of the sordid and the cruel and even blasphemous appear on TV, we do not switch off in a 'holier than thou' spirit. We recognise that they are part of the real world in which we live and in which our own Rule has to be lived out.

Esther de Waal tells us how St. Benedict used to instruct his monks that when they met together for prayer and started with the Gloria... "pray the Gloria very slowly because some people might be late, and although there is a penalty for being late, try to give everyone as much of a chance as possible to escape it!" I love this proper consideration for human failure.

So our Rule is not to be burdensome but it is to be real. It should be inspired by love and by our realising that when we fail, love forgives. There is always the possibility that through forgiven failure we may make progress in the Christian life.

How beautifully and realistically this is expressed by George Herbert:

> *Love bade me welcome; yet my soul drew back,*
> *Guilty of dust and sin.*
> *But quick-eyed love, observing me grow slack*
> *From my first entrance in,*
> *Drew nearer to me, sweetly questioning*
> *if I lacked anything.*
> *"A guest", I answered, "worthy to be here:"*
> *Love said, "You shall be he".*
> *"I, the unkind, ungrateful? Ah, my dear,*
> *I cannot look on Thee."*
> *Love took my hand and smiling did reply,*
> *"Who made the eyes but I?"*
> *"Truth, Lord, but I have marred them; let my shame*
> *Go where it doth deserve.*
> *"And know you not," says Love, "who bore the blame?"*
> *"My dear, then I will serve."*
> *"You must sit down," says Love, "and taste my meat."*
> *So I did sit and eat.*

QUESTIONS FOR DISCUSSION

1. Just how important for our future development are our early childhood years? Share experiences. Do you feel that the way these years influence later life is exaggerated? Discuss ways of helping those who appear insecure and unable to cope. How can we help God's Fatherhood to come alive for them? What helps us to feel that we are loved by God?

2. Do you think that we pay sufficient attention to how we react to the various traumas of life? How much are we influenced by our feelings as distinct from our ability to think rationally? Do we need to be more deliberate about receiving and offering forgiveness? Is corporate confession within worship sufficient to deal with our sins?

3. Discuss the value of a simple Rule. Then devise the outline of a Rule which you think could be a spur to a disciplined discipleship.

Seven daily readings about Discipline

ONE   OBEDIENCE

"Let Christ be the chain that binds you." This was — and is — part of the Benedictine Rule. The question which then arises is: "How do I so interiorise Christ that I am aware of the true nature of 'the chain that binds me'?" The answer is by dwelling regularly on the words and works of Jesus and deliberately asking about the implications of them for our own lives and responsibilities.

Then we have the example of Jesus himself. Alan Dale in his *New World* translation translates *Romans 5:6* in this way: *"So Jesus died at the right time. None of us was strong enough to deal with the mess we had got ourselves into; Jesus gave his life to get us out of it".*

The added bonus is that Jesus is not only an example. Our awareness of his adventurous pioneering leaves us with a sense of aching need. Then the Pioneer comes to our aid because he is also our potential Saviour. The only way in which we can hope to be obedient to the constraints Christ puts upon us is by trusting him to provide the strength to succeed. It was Catherine of Genoa who said: "My me is God nor do I know my selfhood save in him".

Our part is to respond in obedience to the insights that come to us within our devotional meditations. As we do our part, so he does his. Our ability to be obedient is related to his willingness to share his life with us and the Cross is the sign of his dedication to our redemption.

Read Peter's declaration about Jesus in Mark 8:27−35. In my wide-margined Bible I have written about this passage: "First came *recognition* (29). A *response* is then invited and it has to be from the precise situation in which I am; with the *resources* which I have and with the *powers* that I can muster".

TWO   POSSESSIONS

We all have them. Some people have more than others but we all possess some things which are of value. There are also people who matter a great deal to us. If we lost them, either through death or in some other way, we should feel utterly bereft.

Possessions, whether things or people, have to be carefully possessed. We are stewards of our possessions and this implies wise and careful management. We should not treat possessions lightly but seek to use them for our own good and for the good of others.

It all goes wrong when possessions possess us, when the

whole business of increasing our stock of possessions takes over. Then we are lost. Wise people realise that we can never possess anything permanently. There comes the time when all our possessions are of no avail. "There are no pockets in a shroud."

Equally we cannot possess people. Some parents try to possess their children. They want to live again through them and so try to retain influence and control. Sometimes they try to 'buy' them with houses, money, cars. It never works. Far better to recognise with the Psalmist: *"To Yahweh belongs earth and all it holds, the world and all who live in it"* *(Psalm 24:1).*

Read Paul on Christian Giving in 2 Corinthians 8:1 – 9.

Then ask... Why do we give? What do we give? To whom do we give? The answers are all here in this passage.

THREE   TODAY'S THE DAY

We all do it. We wake up and survey what we think the day may bring and say to ourselves: "It's going to be a dull day today; I wish I had something exciting on". We may even wish that day away because tomorrow we have something on that we think will bring colour and variety to our lives.

It is a mistake! Each day has its own peculiar treasure to be discovered and enjoyed. If it so happens that we have got nothing much on, this then provides us with a rare opportunity. We can use the hours to engage in some form of creative activity.

Take a walk alone and make careful notes in your mind of what you hear and see and smell. Look at the delicate veins etched on the leaves. Observe the tiny little bird as it skips from bush to tree. Listen to its gay song. Smell the damp earth. Utilise those powers of observation and hearing you have almost forgotten you possess.

Think of someone who might benefit from seeing you. You know that they are lonely and perhaps depressed. Go and see them and help them to see that they matter; that they are cared for and loved. But be natural about it — and enjoy yourself!

Savour the blessings in a normal day. Remember, *today's the day!*

Read Matthew 6:25-34. Think about and around birds... wild flowers... seeds... food... clothing... anxiety. All life is here but the one slice of it you possess is today! How are you going to spend it? What are you going to look for? Who, among the people you know, needs you most?

FOUR   THE CAVE OF LIVING STREAMS

Ignatius went for a time to live in a cave at Manresa, by the banks of the River Cordoner. He went there at a time of darkness and desolation but he discovered in the cave an experience of illumination and integration.

He then emerged to advocate "contemplation in action" and also "a seeking God in all things". These were two of his living streams.

They can be ours. Contemplation by itself leads to stagnation. It can also deteriorate into day-dreaming. We go into the cave to be quiet and listen. Then when we have heard we come out. But how different life is now!

118

Just how different? This may depend upon our utilising the wisdom of Ignatius and "seeking God in all things".

I am an activist by nature and I have never found solitude easy. But when I began to go into a cave from time to time (in my case a wooden hut in the grounds of a Roman Catholic Community), I discovered things about myself and about God which I am sure gave a new depth to my work and a deeper quality to my relationships.

Read Isaiah 6:1 – 6.
Read John 14:25 – 31.

What adventures, revelations, promises came to the disciples in the Upper Room! Then Jesus said "Come, let us go from this place" (31). This pattern is an essential feature of our disciplined discipleship.

FIVE   TRUE FRIENDSHIP

There are always feelings associated with the important and significant events in life. We usually have no difficulty in sharing our 'nice' feelings. Indeed if something happens to us which gives intense pleasure our friends know that we are feeling good just by looking at us!

But what of life's negative experiences, its disappointments, its failures, being bereaved, losing our job and finding it difficult to get another?

And what about those feelings which arise unasked and uninvited? There seems no obvious external reason for them, but they are there. Sometimes they are associated with difficulties in relationships but we cannot quite understand why such feelings should come over us.

We can try to bury them and tell ourselves that we must keep a stiff upper lip and not give way to ourselves but they will not go away! They will remain and the deeper we drive them down the more destructive they will be. Some day they will erupt — and the results will not be pleasant.

Tell someone you can trust. Be quite frank about your feelings. They may seem to be childish, which is why you have been tempted to keep things to yourself. It is far better to open up. Once they have been expressed, you will feel better and any sense of shame associated with the feelings will begin to disappear. But make sure you get the right person. There are different levels of friendship. It must be someone you can really trust and who is committed to confidentiality.

Read 1 John 1:5 – 10. When you have shared with a friend they may go on to help you to share with God. Does the phrase about having "fellowship with one another" authenticate the above suggestion?

SIX   PRAYING FOR OURSELVES

We should pray for ourselves but we should pray for the right things. It would be wrong in most circumstances to pray for material success; it would be right to pray for forgiveness for ourselves and for our ability to be forgiving to others.

Prayer for ourselves begins in our seeking to be attuned to the Father's mind. This is why regular meditation is important. We are getting deeper into God's mind and thus deeper into our own selves. Eventually we are led to that height where we are just worshipping in silence and being grateful for life and love.

But, on the way, we are entitled to ask for small things. We are small people and we realise our smallness when we open ourselves in the silence to God's greatness. God is mindful of our every condition and he does not despise our sincere petitions although sometimes he will answer our prayers in ways different from our asking.

What is certain is that praying for ourselves will bring greater sensitivity in our relationships and a deeper awareness of the real needs of others. Our efficiency in work and witness will also be enhanced. It pays for ourselves and the 'pay' is in the gold coin of love — given and received.

Read the account of how Jesus prayed for himself in the Garden of Gethsemane in Matthew 26:36 – 46.

Note the honesty of the prayer and note also his use of the phrase, "if it is possible". Note also his words to three of his disciples, "Keep watch and pray so that you will not enter into temptation". A resolute discipline is displayed by Jesus. Sadly a lack of discipline is shown by the three disciples.

SEVEN   THE DISCIPLINE OF BELIEVING

In the introduction to his monumental work, *On Being a Christian*[25], Dr. Hans Küng indicates that, although he hopes his book will be of help, in the end, "each one for himself alone, quite personally, can be or not be a Christian".

You who read these words are very likely to be Christians, those who have deliberately opted to follow Jesus. Even so you must, at least sometimes, wonder about the credibility of the 'good news'. You read a devastating critique of the faith. Your children or close friends raise questions about the validity of believing and the usefulness of church-going. You experience at first hand one of those agonising difficulties of relating the loving purposes of a good God to the awfulness of human suffering. You say to yourself: can it be true?

In fact a mature faith needs to ask questions and wrestle with problems. If it were easy to believe, then faith, as we understand it, would not be necessary.

Küng further suggests that, although we must find our own answers, we do this, not just by awareness of Christian teaching and doctrine, "but by Christian existence, action, conduct".

As so often a quotation from Alan Dale inspires me. *"The secret of splendid living is to stake your life on the beloved son."* My own mind also harmonises with a verse from one of Fred Pratt Green's splendid hymns:

> *In the discipline of praying,*
> *When its hardest to believe;*
> *In the drudgery of caring,*
> *When it's not enough to grieve;*
> *Faith, maturing, learns acceptance*
> *Of the insights we receive.*

Read the story of the solemn interview between Jesus and Peter in John 21:15 – 23. He was told to be a doer of the word and to get on with loving and caring. We know now that he did, and his faith was strengthened.

9 STILLNESS

Let Mother Teresa be our beginning:

> *The fruit of Silence is Prayer,*
> *The fruit of Prayer is Faith,*
> *The fruit of Faith is Love,*
> *The fruit of Love is Service.*

Within these sentences lies a rich pattern of Christian living, and it all begins with being silent, being still. It was Pascal who said that "most of man's troubles come from his not being able to sit quietly in his own room". Modern civilisation seems to have developed an anti-silence drive. Previous generations did not have so many noisy, electronic devices as we have today. The sight of young people on the streets and in buses and trains with their personal stereos suggests that those who use them feel that they must always have sounds ringing in their ears. Whatever happened to reading and just thinking? To fill the ears with a constant cacophony of sound cannot be good for the health of body, mind or spirit.

There is, of course, a difference between silence and stillness. Whilst silence is an essential part of stillness, stillness is not necessarily part of silence. You can be outwardly silent and inwardly seething. Stillness is the fruit of carefully disciplined habits. To discover inward stillness is more important than just being silent, but, it cannot, of course, come without silence so the two experiences are vitally related.

THE EXPERIENCE OF STILLNESS

How can we help ourselves to discover the experience of stillness?

First we do need to *recognise the difficulties*. Our minds are the repositories for a multitude of happenings and events, both positive and negative, going back to the earliest years of our lives. Memories galore are imprinted upon the discs of our own 'personal' computers. We also have an enormous bank of 'feeling' responses, many of which we cannot consciously link with the events which first caused them. Memories and feelings all come back into our consciousness invited and uninvited and the uninvited ones often come at unexpected times.

Dreams are sometimes the vehicle these memories use and they can be forgotten when we awake, but their being rehearsed in this way helps to keep them strongly alive. Within the silence they will always try to invade our stillness because our internal computer discs cannot be erased. This means that we have to find ways of controlling them and devise our own methods of 'centering down' into stillness.

I find that I can do this best by beginning with a few simple exercises combined with controlled breathing. The exercises are simply bringing the different parts of the body into tension and then letting go. The mind also gives orders to the body to relax in sections, usually beginning with toes and feet and working upwards. Controlled breathing means consciously slowing down the breathing rate and making sure that, as we breathe in, we use the whole of our lungs. Fast, shallow breathing can cause hyperventilation which in turn produces undesirable physical effects. Place your hand over the umbilicus and gently resist the swelling of your abdomen. This is where you should be breathing.

Once this is functioning then I use a Bible word or sentence and concentrate upon it. An obvious favourite is... *"Be still... and know... that I am God"* (Psalm 46:10). Another favourite is... *"Mar-an-atha"* which means *"Come, Lord Jesus"*. Ten minutes of this and I begin to feel a sense of stillness within which prompts me to turn to a passage of scripture or to the devotional book I am reading at that time.

124

Reading, contemplating, meditating, praying, are then all combined. Often a verse, thought or idea seems to stand out as being more important than the rest. This is God's word for me that day and is noted in my wide-margined Bible or my prayer diary. This thought will be likely to come back to me from time to time during the day and I try to make sure I think around it last thing at night. It might be just one word like 'grace' for instance. This is an invitation to use my imagination to feel myself surrounded by God's grace which is his love in action and directed towards me. I can visualise it like a blanket of warm air. This adds to my sense of stillness and enhances my security.

Yesterday (as I write) I was with a Franciscan Friar. He told me: "You, or anyone else, can have twenty-three hours of my day if you need me, but my two half-hours of prayer are mine. I will not allow you or anyone else to take them away from me. They are my life-line". What might such experiences do for us?

FAITH WILL BE STRENGTHENED

There has to be an intellectual element in our Christian pilgrimage. The faith by which we live must command the assent of our minds. Blind belief as well as 'blind unbelief' is 'sure to err'. Yet we do not find a mature faith by the process of reason alone.

In the historic interview on BBC television between John Freeman and Professor Carl Jung, there is that tremendous moment when Jung is asked about his belief in God. He only replied after a few moments of awe-inspiring silence. He then said that it was not really a question of belief but "I know!" In the cold light of describing such an incident it could sound like an arrogant reply. Those who saw the interview did not feel that. Prior to the answer there had been an inward wrestling. Then the sheer reality and authenticity of the man broke through in his reply. His sense of 'knowing' was not only due to his intellectual quest, it was the consequence of his explorations of the human psyche and his own awareness of the numinous. His was not an orthodox faith. He did not, so far as I am aware, belong to any particular Church. He knew because he had been 'in the presence' and the ultimate reality he had encountered there was the living God.

Recounting this story does not mean that I believe that our own faith has to be built only on such awareness of God as we may encounter in the stillness. No, not on this alone. But the historic facts of the faith and the affirmations of theology come alive as they are held in creative tension between our experiences in the silence and our action, witness and encounters in the market place.

STILLNESS AND SIMPLICITY

Before Harry Williams became a Monk with the Community of the Resurrection, he was Dean of Trinity College, Cambridge. One day the Queen visited the College. She was attired in a beautiful green dress and Harry Williams commented to the wife of a colleague on how simple a style it seemed to him. Her reply was: "Yes, indeed, but that very simplicity is a sign of the art and skill of her couturier" (her dress designer).

We sometimes use the word 'simple' to describe a person who is mentally retarded. It is a wrong use of the word. To attain to simplicity is to reach a considerable height in the art of being.

The kind of simplicity I discover in the stillness helps me to unravel some of the twists and muddles in which I so easily land myself. Life can be like a ball of string that has been used once and then only loosely put together. As you try to unwind it so it becomes tangled and impossible to use.

If you persevere however, sometimes there is that special moment when with a good shake it becomes untwisted. Now it can be put to its proper use.

I find that happens from time to time with my personal dilemmas. In the stillness it is often the simple thoughts which emerge that are the most creative. I find this also in my public work. I am often dealing with controversial issues on which there are varying points of view. Debate can become quite heated and from time to time I have been known to say: "We are just not listening to each other; let's be quiet and seek God's stillness". I go on to suggest that, on many issues, there is no moral absolute that must be right for everybody in precisely the same way. On some issues what is right for one may well be wrong for another. That which is often enhanced in the silence is mutual respect and trust.

A SIMPLE BASIC TRUTH

Sometimes it is a simple basic truth which comes alive for us in the stillness.

Years ago I was with my family on a beach in the southern state of Louisiana in the USA. It was a warm, sticky, but dull day. We scarcely saw the sun but we sat and bathed and lazed and bathed. As we were driving home, the awful truth dawned upon us that we were all badly sunburnt. The following day it was much worse. Because we could not see it, we thought that the sun was not shining down on us. Yet we were getting literally scorched by the sun's powerful rays.

God's love is always there. What more simple and basic truth is there? If God is and if his nature is love, then that love is ever moving out towards us. The Christian religion has so often been misunderstood as consisting of ideals after which we must strive. We therefore engage in a deadly struggle, trying our best to become what we think God wants us to be. It is as though God is over against us while the simple basic truth is that he is on our side! Paul had to find this out the hard way. So did John Wesley. My own deepest experiences have seldom been in great assemblies. They have happened in the stillness when I have been alone with God, or they have happened in the closeness of an intimate relationship with someone I love, and who has come to mean much to me.

STILLNESS AND VALUES

How easy it is to be pressured into adopting the values society tries to impose upon me. The values associated with appearance, possessions, impressive homes and so on, the 'razmataz' of banquets, parties, lavish entertainment, fast cars. All these are presented as necessary features of "the good life". As I recall memories of simple packed lunches eaten on the top of mountains with good friends with whom I have shared in pleasant conversation, I feel that I know where the real treasure of life is to be found. As I sit quietly inside the Chapel of a Community of those I have come to love for their simple lifestyle and for their deep sharing and real caring, I believe that I am in touch with the riches which are beyond price. All these things are in some way associated with stillness. Yes, I love company; I love my wife and family and I like to be with them. But I also like to be alone... in the stillness... in the silence... for there God is to be found and greater meaning is given to the mystery we call life.

STILLNESS AND SACRAMENT

When I am celebrating Holy Communion or participating in a sacramental service, I like to encourage, and have the opportunity to participate in, an experience of stillness. When I am giving the bread and wine to others, I like them to look up and meet my eyes. As I give the bread I make sure that I touch the hand of those receiving. Few words are needed. It is the intention which matters. These are high moments of devotional experience.

When you come to think about it the Lord's Supper was originally part of an ordinary meal. The bread was the same as that which they had already eaten at supper. The wine was part of that which they had already drunk. The cup was the ordinary means of drinking. Holy Communion is at the heart of worship. Let it be celebrated "decently and in order", but let it be simple.

The structure of the Communion Service contains within it all the elements which go to make up a meaningful life. There is thankfulness and praise (the Gloria); Penitence and the deep expression of sorrow for sin (Confession); the direct assurance of forgiveness; loving fellowship (The Peace); Petition — asking God to be truly present in bread and wine; and when the service is over, a new start. As Fred Kaan puts it in one of his hymns:

> Now let us from this table rise
> Renewed in body, mind and soul;
> With Christ we die and live again,
> His selfless love has made us whole.

I have come to see the value of drawing out what is already actively present in every Service of Holy Communion and that is its healing potential. As we have seen, all the wholesome, life-giving factors are there. How good and wise it is to suggest that the bread and wine, the signs of the "real presence" should be directed towards those points in our lives where there is a real need. As an older hymn writer, Henry Twells, put it:

> Thy touch has still its ancient power.

STILLNESS PERVADES ACTIVITY

What I have been trying to express through this chapter is that stillness is an attitude of mind as well as a response to a disciplined habit. Our special times of quiet and stillness are necessary for us to call up those inward resources whenever we need them most. And that is often in the hurly-burly of decision-making and practical Christian service.

Happily there are many signs that people are beginning to tire of a consumer oriented society and want to return to more simple values. This is evidenced by the rise of the Green movement and the desire to revert to more natural methods of farming and gardening, the increase in vegetarianism and lifestyles which fit in more easily with the rhythm of nature. God is at work quietly in our midst and, in the end, the search for simplicity is part of our search for meaning and purpose and so part of our search for God.

I realise that I often refer to Alan Dale. I only met him once but he was as I expected, 'laid back', in control, resourceful, aware, sensitive. Living with the scriptures for so long had made a profound impression upon him. This is revealed in so many of his inspired translations both of the New and Old Testaments. Let this chapter end with two appropriate quotations from *New World:*

Give your minds to what is true, noble, right and clean, lovely and graceful. Wherever you find excellence — things worth getting excited about — concentrate on them.

Master every situation with the quietness of heart which Jesus gives you. This is how you were meant to live; not each by himself but together in company with all the friends of Jesus.

QUESTIONS FOR DISCUSSION

1. Share your own experiences of seeking for inner quiet and stillness. Do not hesitate to tell each other about

130

your difficulties. What practical helps or devices have you found useful in addition to those suggested in this chapter?

2. Has the rise of the 'Green' movement and the new emphasis upon organically produced food affected you in any way? Does our Christian witness require of us that we think more about the way we use (or abuse) 'the good earth'? Have your own personal ways of life been affected?

3. Does participation in Holy Communion (The Eucharist) nourish your inner being? The answer may seem obvious but be honest about it. Are there any ways of celebrating the Sacrament which you find more helpful than others? Does the idea of directing a particular Celebration towards a specific need appeal to you?

Note:
Consider ending this group session with ten minutes of silence in which you seek an individual and corporate sense of stillness.

Seven daily readings about Stillness

ONE   PRAYING WITH THE PSALMS

I have often worshipped with the Franciscan Friars and been intrigued by their regular use of the Psalms. They have a particular way of chanting them with a little pause between each sentence. Initially I found the practice rather dull, even boring. I shared my feelings with Brother Bernard, at that time the Guardian of the Friary. "Let the words flow over you", he suggested. "Don't try to hold on to every thought but grasp hold of just one or two. There is everything you need in the Psalms for your soul's good."

Of course there is.

Bearing fruit (1)
Trust (3,4 and 11)
Pleading (6)
Folly (12)
Cry for help (17)
Feeling forsaken (22)
Guidance (23)

All these varying emotions, feelings, thoughts, ideas are repeated again and again. Sometimes however a different note is struck:

Anger (88)
Anguish (120)

As part of your devotional pattern try taking at least one Psalm each week and, after 'centering down', pick out thoughts which have impressed you and apply them to your own real life situation.

Like my Franciscan friends you will discover that the Psalms are an indispensable devotional tool... because... *"Through thy precepts I get understanding... and... Thy word is a lamp unto my feet and a light to my path". (Psalm 119:104 and 105)*

TWO   THE GLORY OF THE LORD

As a small boy I recall my Mother going round the house singing this verse of a hymn:

> *O that will be, glory for me,*
> *Glory for me, Glory for me;*
> *When, by his grace, I shall look on his face,*
> *That will be glory, be glory for me.*

I did not wonder about it at the time but I have often wondered since about the word 'glory'. What does it mean?

I gained a little insight when I read *The Wind in the Willows*. Rat and Mole had set out before dawn to search for the baby Otter who had been lost for several days:

> *"This is the place of my song dream, the place where the music played to me," whispered the Rat as if in a trance. "Here in this holy place, here if anywhere surely we shall find him!"*

> *Then suddenly the Mole felt a great awe fall upon him, an awe that turned his muscles to water, bowed his head and rooted his feet to the ground. It was no panic terror — indeed he felt wonderfully at peace and happy — but it was an awe that smote and held him and, without seeing, he knew that it could only mean that some august presence was very near... "Rat," he found breath to whisper, "are you afraid?"*

> *"Afraid", murmured the Rat, his eyes shining with unutterable love. "Afraid of him? Oh never, never! And yet — and yet Oh Mole, I am afraid!"*

> *Then the two animals crouching to the earth, bowed their heads and did worship.*

Now read the Transfiguration Story in Matthew 17:1–13. Imagine yourself there. Martin Luther King was able to say, "I have seen the glory". Have you?

From time to time in history God seems to choose someone through whom he reveals himself to others in special ways. Thomas Merton was such a person. Through his many writings he has become a spiritual director to thousands and thousands. His premature death as the result of an accident in Bangkok seems to have given an added authority to what he wrote.

He was, from time to time, a hermit, living entirely alone. But out of his solitariness emerged his compassion which Monica Furlong (in her biography entitled simply *Merton*[26] described as "Overflowing in a huge longing to help humanity in the agonising effort to build a world that contained love and justice and peace".

Merton appeals to me because his saintliness was always 'earthy'. He was not afraid to reveal his humanity. He was a whole person whose inner wounds contributed towards his wholeness. He would not have cast his spell upon people as he did if he had not been as transparently authentic as he surely was.

A fellow Monk who belongs to the same Trappist Order. Father Basil Pennington has written *A Retreat with Thomas Merton*[27] (Amity House USA 1988). In it he imagines what Merton might have said if he had been able to leave one final message:

> Live the questions. There is struggle all the way. Be free! Be yourself! How? By Prayer. I don't mean saying prayers. I mean prayer where you leave all your thoughts and images behind... and find your true self in God. At the same time we find everybody else there. And we realise that we are all one in God and everything else follows.

Read John 17 and dwell upon the relationship Jesus had with his disciples. You are one of them now and he is praying for you (verse 20). I sometimes suggest we translate verse 11 as "That they might be *whole*, even as we are *whole*". I think Merton might have approved that!

FOUR   OPEN TO GOD

Brother Ramon, a Franciscan Friar, has spent two periods living entirely alone. Each has lasted for six months and both have proved creative in his own life and, through his writings, particularly creative in the lives of others.

He explained his reasons for setting out on his first venture in a letter to his friends and prayer supporters. He was going in response to a sense of inward constraint and he believed that it would be for him... "an affirmation of the primacy of God's love". He realised that it would be a wilderness experience and that he would be subjected to particular temptations, but he believed that his membership of the Franciscan brotherhood and the prayer support of his friends would enable him to survive and to benefit from the experience.

He devised for himself (with the help of his Guardian) a programme of liturgical prayer, study (including writing) and manual work (a big vegetable patch), but insisted that all these would, from time to time, be laid aside "for the sake of silence and prayer".

There is no doubt that God used this time of solitariness to deepen Ramon's experience and to enable him to communicate it to others through the spoken and written word.

Is God calling you to undertake some form of Retreat when, in the silence you become especially 'open to God'? Or is God calling you so to order your days that you utilise the silence of the early morning hour? You will need your own structure but, like Ramon, you will need liturgy, scripture, silent meditation, stillness, response to God (perhaps written). The Retreat and/or these early morning hours could bring you closer to God and enable you to become more useful to others.

Now read 1 Kings 19:11–13 and follow this up with a look at Luke 4:42. If Jesus needed to 'go apart', so do we.

FIVE   HELP FROM JUNG

In the text of this chapter we mentioned the famous interview between Carl Jung and John Freeman. One of the central features of Jung's teaching was his desire to help people forward into psychological and emotional maturity by the process he called *individuation*. There are elements in this process which are sound gospel truths:

Acceptance

Jung helped people to accept themselves honestly. This meant being aware of one's own limitations but acknowledging also one's creative energies.

Jesus accepted people as they were. He made this clear with a man like Zacchaeus *(see Luke 19:1–10)* and in words like those in *John 6:37: "Him that cometh to me I will in no wise cast out"*.

However his acceptance of the total person included their strenths as well as their weaknesses. Jesus told us to love our neighbours *as ourselves* (Mark 12:31). So we must love all of ourselves because that is what God does. Individuation for

Jung meant growth and development leading to a greater integration or personal wholeness.

Realisation

Basic truths about life have to be realised in experience. Jung wanted people to reach various stages in the journey of life where they made creative leaps forward. The good news of the gospel goes much further. It offers a power to enable this forward movement of the human spirit. The process is called sanctification or growth in holiness. There are resources avilable to us through prayer and a trusting attitude of life which makes this possible. The gospel insight is that God is alive and active in his world prompting this activity. He takes the initiative and then invites our response. *"We love because God first loved us"* (1 John 4:19).

SIX   HELP FROM WILLIAM TEMPLE

The one-time Archbishop of Canterbury, William Temple, had many wise things to say about prayer and worship and he still helps many of us in our inward searchings through his *Readings in St. John's Gospel*[28]. Two of his sayings about worship may help us towards new attitudes to worship ourselves. The sayings are:

> *It is not that conduct is the end of life and worship helps it but that worship is the end of life and conduct tests it.*
>
> *The world will be saved by worship.*

It is a little difficult to realise the truth of these sayings. Worship often seems to be divorced from life. It takes place in special buildings and employs special rituals and ceremonies and requires special people to give a lead.

But this is only one aspect of worship. When we worship, we are declaring what we believe to be the most valuable things in life. We offer them to God in our prayers and he responds with his love and grace directly in relation to those items to which we give priority.

I once had, in my congregation, a high powered civil servant who reported directly to his particular government minister. One Sunday I noticed that he was in his place as usual. At that time his department was under severe pressure and his activities were the subject of press speculation. I foolishly said to him on the way out that I thought he might have been having to wrestle with affairs of state that day. His reply was, "Where do you think I get the strength I need for my wrestling?" I felt suitably admonished and humbled.

Read Ephesians 5:18–20 and Revelation 21:1–4.

SEVEN   SANCTIFIED IMAGINATION

I belong to a Cancer Self-Help Support Group. One of the ways which we use to help each other is by the use of sanctified imagination. We engage in simple relaxation exercises and then have a time of meditation. Those who are in the midst of cancer treatment visualise healing streams coming towards them at the point of their need. Those of us who do not have cancer think of them each in turn. We hold them up in God's love and care and we also build up a picture of God's healing streams being focussed on their needs.

Those who have cancer say that it helps. We who do not have cancer feel that it is a privilege to be with them and to surround them with our love as well as attempting to be channels of God's love.

138

We are not all committed Christians who attend the group. Many are, but others are searching. I go one step further in my use of sanctified imagination. I build up a picture of Jesus and see him by the side of each of them in turn. His hands are stretched out towards them and laid upon their heads. I know that others do the same.

This way of praying for others is often right when we are involved with them in their dilemmas, when we are trying to help them to locate the source of a particular problem which has plagued them for years. Often it goes back to an incident which caused them deep hurt; perhaps rejection; perhaps being wronged by another in an aggressive way. It happened years ago and has been buried. Now, in the present, we recognise that it is still hurting and the hurt is harmful.

So we say to them: "Let's be quiet... Relax... God is here... Build up a picture of Jesus... See him moving towards a needy person in the New Testament... Now see him moving towards you... Feel the hurt... Live through it but remember... Jesus is with you... His hands are upon you... He offers you forgiveness and invites you to be forgiving to those others who were involved... Be quietly thankful for the blessings received."

Read Ephesians 3:14 – 21. Note especially Paul's prayer, which includes his petition that *"God will give you power through his Spirit to be strong in your inner selves... and that Christ will make his home in your hearts"*.

10 LOVE

This final chapter is different. It it centred around the events of Holy Week and picks out eight significant words each of which highlights one aspect of the love demonstrated by Jesus during this last, incident packed week. The meditations which follow are also different. Read the chapter right through first. There is much material for group activity as well as personal reflection but within groups let the emphasis be on *sharing*. You will have noticed that I have tried to stimulate sharing through the questions suggested following each chapter. Holy Week is however special and sharing is an essential part of our response to these moving events. Then additionally you could take one of the words each day throughout the week and link them with the suggested Bible readings and prose-poem style meditations.

1 Gratitude

Yes, people were grateful for the words and works of Jesus. Unwelcome authority (Jewish and Roman) had been challenged. The sick had been healed. Wisdom for living had been offered in story and pithy saying. Their 'Hosannas' were sincere. Their gratitude was real.

Nevertheless they not fully understood the nature of his love. Many of them thought that he was instigating an uprising against Rome. They had to discover later that he had chosen a very different path. It was this path that many couldn't accept. Hence their faithlessness. Some who shouted 'Hosanna' on the first Palm Sunday were the same people who shouted 'Crucify' on the following Friday.

Do not blame them too much. We live with hindsight. They did not have the whole picture. Now take an example from their gratitude. Get in touch with your own indebtedness to Jesus. Think about the ways he has influenced your life. Recall recent blessings. Even if you are passing through difficult times, there are things to be grateful for in the past — and perhaps for sustaining help in the present.

Sincere gratitude will lead to Praise — and Praise is a healthy exercise.

2 Grief

On Palm Sunday the grief was his. As he rounded a bend on his way up the Mount of Olives, suddenly the city was before him. There were the homes of the people he loved. Feeling already the pangs of rejection "Jesus wept". I recall looking through the famous Chalice Window in the Church of Dominus Flevit. Through this window is the same view of the old City of Jerusalem that Jesus saw. I recall how we tried to lay hold of his grief.

Grief comes from many different sources, but particularly through the loss of those we dearly love. But this is not the only kind of grief. We can grieve over wrongdoing as Jesus did. We can properly be sad about the many manifestations of evil which surround us in this present world.

It was not only faith and courage which brought the Salvation Army into being. It was also grief. General William Booth expressed it this way:

> While women weep as they do now, I'll fight; while men go to prison, in and out, in and out, I'll fight; while there is one poor lost girl on the streets, I'll fight; while there remains one dark soul without the light of God, I'll fight — I'll fight to the very end.

Don't be afraid to grieve — but don't bury yourself in any kind of grief. There are people who need what only you can do for them — and the Bible requires us all so to be involved as to "share Christ's sufferings" (1 Peter 4:13).

3 Anger

We had an initial look at Anger in the chapter on 'Problems'; now we look at it again within the context of Holy Week. Anger was closely related to grief in the experience of Jesus. He was sad about what he saw happening in the Temple, but he was also angry. It was his anger which spilled over into action. Out they had to go — the slick salesmen and the money lending sharks. This was not what the Temple was for; it was for prayer and thanksgiving.

Anger needs to be expressed. Great harm can come from repressing anger. But its expression must never be in vicious retribution. *"An eye for an eye and a tooth for a tooth"* was the old law which Jesus superseded with the law of love. But love does not outlaw anger; as we have seen, Jesus could be angry. But ultimately he wanted what was best for everybody. He knew that anger which attempts to destroy may well turn out to destroy the destroyer. The kind of anger Jesus expressed was justified because he lived and died to right wrongs and defeat evil.

Archbishop Tutu is an angry man. He hates apartheid but he does not hate those who want to maintain its unjust laws and regulations. He wants to see them change. His anger is redemptive. The poet, Stevie Smith expresses it in this way:

> *Anger it was that won him hence,*
> *As only anger taught him sense.*
> *Often my tears fall in a shower*
> *Because of anger's freeing power.*

You may be angry in a just cause — but do not let the sun go down on your wrath! *(See Romans 12:9−21.)*

4 Conflict

Throughout Holy Week there was conflict. There was conflict between Jesus and his disciples; they did not want him to die on a cross. There was conflict between Jesus and the Jewish authorities; they wanted him dead because they felt threatened by him. There was conflict between the Jews and Pilate; he really did not want to condemn Jesus to be crucified but he was placed under such intense pressure that he felt he had to do so. Jesus said that there would be conflict: *"Do not think I have come to bring peace to the world; no, I did not come to bring peace but a sword"* (Matthew 10:34). In the Christian life it is possible to mistake health for disease. Conflicts can be destructive but, rightly handled, they can be life-giving.

No one knew the reality of conflict better than Dietrich Bonhoeffer. He wrestled within himself about becoming involved in the plot to kill Hitler but decided that he should. When the plot failed he was sent to prison and ultimately he was executed. When he was near the end he wrote a poem entitled *Stations on the Road to Freedom*. Those stations were:

Discipline "Only through discipline may a man learn to be free!"

Action "Daring to do what is right, not what fancy may tell you!"

Suffering "A change has come indeed, your hands, so strong and active, are bound."

Death "Come now, thou greatest of feasts on the journey to freedom eternal, cast aside all the burdensome chains."

Out of that conflict came a powerful testimony and living theological concepts which brought liberation to many Christians, and not a few would-be Christians who passed through doubt to faith.

5 Identification

Each Maundy Thursday the team of priests in a Roman Catholic Parish in Paris moves among the congregation,

143

each with basin, water and towel. They wash and dry the feet of everyone present. Then each in turn makes confession to the members of the congregation and the congregation corporately pronounces absolution. In this way they identify with the people. They are saying that, although their roles may be different within the Church of Christ, liturgically and spiritually they belong together.

Jesus identified himself with the people to whom he came in a variety of ways. *"He was tempted in all parts like as we are..."* (Hebrews 4:15). *"He was the 'Good Shepherd' who gave his life for the sheep"* (John 10:11).

> *He came down to earth from heaven,*
> *Who was God and Lord of all.*
> (C. F. Alexander)

Incarnation implied identification. Just as he identified with us and our spiritual poverty and need, so the call to discipleship involves our identification with people in their needs. Being one with them; sharing their real life experiences.

Evangelism which sees people as fish to be caught out of their natural habitat and hauled aboard the Good Ship Salvation lacks an important element, that of identification. Evangelism which gets alongside people with something to share pays richer dividends. Research in the USA indicates that the overwhelming number of people from outside the Church who come and remain, do so because someone from within identified with them and became their friend. Around us all the time are people who are wide open to gospel truth. They are waiting for someone to care.

6 Sacrifice

> *Thou, O my Jesus, thou didst me*
> *Upon the cross embrace;*
> *For me didst bear the nails and spear,*
> *And manifold disgrace.*

144

So runs a verse from the 17th century. The sacrifice on Calvary was made so many years ago that its relevance to life today is easily lost. The event which has brought about a transformation in the hearts of millions can so easily degenerate into sentiment. Some hymns even seem to assist this process.

Men and women still die for others. Jan Palach sets himself alight in Prague to protest against a flagrant abuse of power. A Chinese student offers flowers to a tank commander and is ground into the dust. Captain Oates walks out into the cold Arctic night in the hope that his friends will be saved. These are stories of sacrifice, but there is one big difference. We cannot always explain it satisfactorily, and as many times as people try they come up with different explanations, but in some strange and mystical way Christ's sacrifice atones for our sins, yours and mine (as Charles Wesley wrote):

> *The bleeding sacrifice*
> *In my behalf appears.*

It was Sidney Carton who took Marnay's place in Charles Dickens' *A Tale of Two Cities*. Carton did it for love of Marnay's wife, Lucy and her child. Dickens wrote that "Carton's face was the peacefullest man's face ever beheld in that place of blood. For sheer love he died instead of Marnay".

Thus in fiction one human being died for another. In reality on the cross (as again Charles Wesley wrote):

> *For all my Lord was crucified,*
> *For all, for all, my Saviour died.*

7 Waiting

In those hours between Good Friday and Easter morning today, we wait. It was not so for those who had seen him die on that first Good Friday; they thought it was the end. Now

145

we wait "in sure and certain hope" for the bright morning.

A brother minister was dying of cancer. In the final weeks of his life he gained great help from a book by W. H. Vanstone. Its title? *The Stature of Waiting*[29].

As I write I have to prepare some notes about Euthanasia for a committee. In few circumstances can there be any justification in cutting a life short by active intervention. There is every justification (I believe) for not prolonging life artificially and even hastening its end by what you do *not* do and by increasing doses of pain relieving drugs.

The Hospice movement is however, the most powerful argument against Euthanasia. In a Hospice patients are helped to die with dignity. A Hospice is a waiting room for death but not in any sad and dreary sense. A modern Hospice is a place where life's ultimate reality is faced with hope, courage — and faith. Many testify to precious days and weeks of "waiting". New discoveries are made and love is discovered and often expressed as never before. When Bishop John Robinson, the author of *Honest to God*, was told that he had six months to live, he set out with his wife to do all the things he had wanted to do but had never had the opportunity to do. It was a time of waiting — but it was also a time of enrichment and personal growth.

8 Victory

> *They pass through the valley of tears*
> *And they make it a place of springs.*
> (Psalm 84:6)

Tears of sadness flowed freely on Good Friday. Tears also flowed on Easter Sunday — but they were tears of joy. This is the Easter message and the consequence of it is that (as Alan Dale translates it):

> *We look at everything differently now;*
> *the hard time we are going through*
> *and the very earth we live on.*

146

We see it all in the light of the
glorious future God will give us.

It was the 'end' which made sense of the beginning. I recall how it helped my thinking when I was enabled to see that the gospels are all resurrection documents. Those who wrote them had shared in the experience of resurrection. This fact coloured the ways in which they wrote about the birth, life and teaching of Jesus.

This opened doors for me. The followers of Jesus must often have been puzzled by his words and actions. He was no 'ordinary' Messiah. He did not fit in with their standard expectations. The resurrection helped them to put the pieces together. Now it all made sense. How can we share their confidence and participate in their experience?

We can do it by recognising that when we launch out and act upon our faith, insights we are given are a taste of resurrection experiences. When we practise love, even when it is hard and difficult, we find ourselves coming to life!

This is what helps us to look forward to the future. If he makes it possible for us to rise up and live now, he will surely take care of the future. This then is what he offers us — the ability to live 'more splendidly' with the help of Jesus, both now and then.

Brother Roger of Taizé in *Praying Together*[30] invites us to pray with him:

> *O Risen Christ,*
> *you breathe your Holy Spirit upon us*
> *like a gentle breeze*
> *and you tell us: "Peace be yours".*
> *Opening ourselves to your peace,*
> *letting it penetrate the harsh and*
> *rocky ground of our hearts*
> *means preparing ourselves to be bearers of*
> *reconciliation wherever you may place us.*
> *But you know that at times we are at a loss.*

147

So come and lead us to wait in silence,
to let a ray of hope shine through in our world.

QUESTIONS FOR DISCUSSION

1. Let members of the group who are willing describe how they lived through the experiences suggested by the eight words. Which experiences came most naturally to you? Do we encourage participants in public worship to get into touch with their feelings?

2. We are often exhorted by church leaders to be more outgoing in our evangelism and to be more ready to invite others to Christian commitment. In the light of Holy Week and our consideration of the gospel of love, how do we feel about how we participate in evangelistic activities?

3. How do we experience resurrection now? Share happenings in your own lives when you "came to life". Are secular experiences of "waking up" to some new aspect of life relevant?

A suggestion End this session by reading corporately out loud the prose poem for Easter Sunday, "The Living Come to Life".

Eight daily readings for Holy Week

INTRODUCTION

In my own preparation for these readings I have concentrated on John's Gospel. It is difficult to piece together the exact

148

sequence of events in this tremendous week and I have not tried to do that. Traditionally, however, some events are wedded to certain days and I have kept to these. On other days I have selected passages from St John which relate to events intimately associated with the passion of our Lord.

In many ways Holy Week is like any other week. We have our work to do, meals to prepare, people to care for. But in a very real way it is different. It is special because the events mark the climax of the earthly ministry of Jesus. It is significant that all the gospel-writers give a large amount of space to tell the story of this week. It was obviously to them a week of supreme importance.

The style of these meditations is a little different from most of the others. I have read and re-read the scripture passage and then let my mind and imagination have free rein. I offer them to you in the hope that they will encourage you, and perhaps enable you, to do the same.

Have a blessed Holy Week.

Read John 12:12–19.

Lazarus had come to life,
the prophet had done it again!
Lepers whole, blind see;
deaf hear; lame walk.

Jesus was his name —
miracle worker.

I must be on the band-wagon;
he might even see me waving —
and that would be good for me —
when the Kingdom comes!

Here he is! Hallelujah!
Look this way, Jesus.

He accepted their praises but —
deep inside was an empty space.
Did they know what he really wanted?
Would they be loyal when the big challenge came?

Will I? Will you?

He "set his face steadfastly to go towards Jerusalem".

Lord, make thy way, my way.

Read John 17:1 – 23.

Jesus prayed.

If he needed to pray for grace and strength
and power to live —
then so must I.

Jesus prayed for his disciples.

To them he had entrusted the word of life —
and to proclaim that word as it should be told,
was never easy.

Nor is it today; to tell it in all its fulness.

But Jesus prayed for his disciples and so,
Jesus prays for us.

For me?

Today?

Yes! Yes! Yes!

And also for those who come alive when they
hear and discover for themselves his way,
his truth, his life.

Jesus prays for us all. He is on our side.
The thrust of life is in his direction.

Mind you — we are still in the world with all
its evil and we are surrounded by temptation.
He will not take us out of the world but,
whilst still living here, he will be with us.

And pray for us. It is enough. Thank you, Lord Jesus.

Read John 13:21 — 38.

Judas was his name.
And the name lives for ever.

His mind was made up. Jesus must either
show his hand or go under. The test would come
when he was arrested.

So Judas arranged it.

As he sped to his fateful task,
told by Jesus to be quick about it;
he left behind a room bathed in light,
for Jesus was (and is) the "light of the world".

The gospel-writer was inside that room — looking out.
He held that awful moment in his mind and
delivered it to posterity in a single sentence:

"It was night!"

Our lives are hinged twixt light and darkness;
we also have a choice

To live our lives inside the room with Jesus,
where it is light.
Or to wander off into the labyrinthine ways,
where all is darkness.

The light will guide us but it will also
reveal our sin.

Judas was his name,
And the name lives for ever.

Read John 13:1−17.

It was good to be with friends,
in that quiet, upper room.
The table was spread with food and drink,
and, best of all, Jesus was with us.

We had travelled over dusty roads
and our feet were soiled and dirty.

Suddenly – it happened – he – Jesus – our Master –
was washing our feet.

What we had been too proud to do,
he did.

None of us ever forgot that moment and, in all
the years ahead, we remembered what he had done,
that night.

Today, someone who is feeling 'soiled'
is looking for a friend.

Today, someone whose life journey has just turned sour,
awaits your call.

Take towel and basin with you for, after all,
disciples are servants!

Read John 15:1—17.

I take hold of the branch,
it feels strong and supple.
I rest my whole weight upon it.
The branch holds.

But here on the ground,
beneath my feet — another branch.
I pick it up. It snaps sharply and lies
broken in my hand.

Why should one be strong and full of life —
and the other ready for the fire?

The reason is plain:
the one is held and life flows from the roots,
through the trunk, to the branches.

The other is dead because it has become
separated from the trunk.

How do I remain alive with his life?

"This is my body, broken for you."

"This is my blood, shed for you."

These glorious gifts you offer me —
that your life may be in me and that
my life may be full.

So am I 'held'.

So shall I live!

Read John 19:17–27.

Pilot gave the order,
unwillingly.

Jesus offered his life,
freely.

The soldiers gambled for his robe,
excitedly.

Jesus beheld his Mother and the disciple John,
lovingly.

His enemies watched him die,
gladly.

Pilate is remembered
as a pliable tool.

Jesus is adored,
because he loved and loves.

The soldiers are remembered
sympathetically.

Jesus' care for his Mother is recalled,
gratefully.

Out of gratitude there still can come:

Love, care, sacrifice, integrity.

So Calvary lives on!

Read John 19:38–42.

Two men in high places,
buried his body.

Joseph of Arimathea loved him,
but his love was not big enough to take risks;
he did not want to tangle with the establishment.

Nicodemus also followed Jesus —
but with reservations — he too lived with fear;
to company with Jesus was dangerous —
so he came to him by night.

As they prepared his body for burial,
their hearts were heavy.
They knew that even this loving care
could not make up for what might have been.

Still, they did what they could and —
engraved their names in history.

Lord, we too feel the pressures of the world;
they try to squeeze us into worldly shapes.
Like these two we enjoy prestige and status,
and do not want to let them go.

So we compromise.

(Of course secrecy is no longer necessary;
the followers of Jesus are respectable nowadays.)

Lord give us the courage to be,
your men and women.
And to let others know gladly,
we are your disciples.

Read John 20:1 – 18.

Mary Magdalene had reason to love Jesus;
he had lifted her from shame to modest pride.
Her life was his; now he had died,
but deep inside she knew: he still held the key.

She came early to his resting place;
he was not there!
She ran to tell his friends — now hers also,
that they had taken him away.

They came and went.
The excitement grew.
Words he had spoken in life —
were now remembered.

Mary was not excited
she felt lost and lonely.
In her bewilderment,
she just wandered here and there.

Then it happened:
was it? could it be? surely it was impossible!

Yes, it was him. He was alive — and Mary came to life
again.

Lord, at times, I too feel lost, bewildered, anxious,
afraid.
Come rise within this life of mine and make me
strong.
Help me to die to sin and rise with you —
to everlasting life!

List of books mentioned in the text

Title	Author	Publisher	Date
1. Julian of Norwich	Grace Jantzen	SPCK	1987
2. Precarious Living	Martin Israel	Hodder & Stoughton	1976
3. Into the New Age	Stephen Verney	Collins/ Fontana	1976
4. Spiritual Man in a New Age	Peter Spink	DLT	1980
5. Watching for Wings	Roger Grainger	DLT	1979
6. The Second Journey	Gerald O'Collins	Villa Books, Dublin	1979
7. The Prophet	Khalil Gilbran	Heinneman	1926
8. The Revelation of Divine Love	Julian of Norwich	Penguin	1966
9. The Significance of Jesus	W. R. Maltby	SCM	1938
10. Tools for Meditation	J. de Rooy	Grail	1970
11. The Wounded Healer	Henri Nouwen	Doubleday	1972
12. The Diseases of Civilisation	Brian Inglis	Hodder & Stoughton	1981
13. Many Voices — One Voice	Eddie Askew	Leprosy Mission	1985
14. Treatise on the Love of God	Francis de Sales		1616
15. A Coat of Many Colours	Michael Wilson	Epworth	1988
16. A Dictionary of Christian Spirituality	ed. Wakefield	SCM	1983
17. The Integrity of Personality	Anthony Storr	Penguin	1960
18. Markings	Dag Hammarskold	Knopf USA	1964
19. The True Wilderness	Harry Williams	Constable	1965
20. Man's Search for Meaning	Viktor Frankl	Hodder & Stoughton	1964
21. Travelling In	Monica Furlong	Hodder & Stoughton	1971
22. Where New Winds Blow	William Hewlett	The Way	1974
23. Summons to Life	Martin Israel	Hodder & Stoughton	1974

158

	Title	Author	Publisher	Date
24.	Seeking God	Esther de Waal	Collins/Fount	1984
25.	On Being a Christian	Hans Küng	Collins	1985
26.	Merton	Monica Furlong	Collins	1980
27.	A Retreat with Thomas Merton	Father Basil Rennington	Amity House, USA	1988
28.	Readings in St John's Gospel	William Temple	McMillan	1950
29.	The Stature of Waiting	W. H. Vanstone	DLT	1982
30.	Praying Together	Brother Roger of Taizé	Mowbray	1982